BROKEN

TIMELINES

Book 3: The Indo-Europeans and Harappans

JACK STORNOWAY

Copyright

BROKEN TIMELINES - BOOK 3: THE INDO-EUROPEANS AND HARAPPANS

First edition. December 29, 2019

Copyright © 2019 Jack Stornoway

ISBN: 978-1990289965

Table of Contents

TABLE OF CONTENTS

Introduction

The Indus Valley Civilization also called the Harappan civilization, is one of the world's foundational cultures, which existed in the territory of modern countries of Pakistan and northwest India, at approximately the same time as the Sumerian and Akkadian civilizations in Mesopotamia, and the Old and Middle Kingdoms in Egypt. The civilization is generally accepted as being a land where an ancient Dravidian language was spoken, likely related to ancient Elamite which was spoken in southern Iran at the time. Several similar depictions of gods or heroes have been found in the ruins of Sumer and the Indus Valley Civilization, which proves significant contact between the cultures, and provides a rough timeline for the Harappan Civilization. These artifacts can either be correlated to the conventional or universal timelines.

Recent DNA evidence has proven the Indo-Iranian peoples had started settling in the Indus Valley Civilization between 2800 and 2300 BC,[1] which means the conventional Harappan timeline either needs to be changed or change the traditional view that the Harappans were Dravidians to Indo-Aryans. This would also require adjusting the view of the Elamites and Sumerians, who both appear to have been closely related to the Harappans. However, Sumerian has never been considered an Indo-European language, let alone an Indo-Aryan language. If the Harappans were Indo-Aryans, then the Sumerian

---

[1]Michael Price (2019) "Genome of nearly 5000-year-old woman links modern Indians to ancient civilization," *American Association For the Advancement of Science*, September 5, 2019

and Elamite languages would need to show the influence of Sanskrit, which they do not. Furthermore, if the Indo-Aryans were the Harappans then the Vedic texts would have been written in South Asia, yet there is no evidence of horses in South Asia until after the fall of the Indus Civilization.

Like the Conventional Egyptian (CET) and Mesopotamian (CMT) Timelines, the Conventional Harappan Timeline (CHT) is impossible to synchronize with the archaeological, linguistic, and genetic evidence. Likewise, the expected length of time that the Sanskrit language took to evolve through its various dialects is also forced into an artificially short period of at most 1200 years, instead of the 3000 to 4000 years generally estimated by linguists. This shorter Indo-European Timeline is referred to herein as the Conventional Indo-European Timeline (CIET), however, unlike the other conventional timelines, the CIET is highly debated among archaeologists, linguists, and geneticists. Currently, several frameworks exist for the development and migrations of the Indo-European tribes, with proposed homelands in either the steppes of Eurasia or the Armenian Highlands, although the steppes have been preferred for the past three decades due to the number of archaeological sites discovered in the region. The framework proposed for the Universal Long Timeline herein is based around the more recent archaeological discoveries across the steppes.

Part 1: Historic Era

Some of the oldest known texts have survived in South Asia, including the *Vedas*, *Avesta*, and Hindu Epics. Most of these texts are believed to have originated outside of South Asia, including the oldest *Vedas*, and the *Avesta*. The *Avesta* was used in Persia by Zoroastrians before they migrated into India after the Islamic conquest of Persia. Most of the Avestan texts no longer exist, as Alexander the Great destroyed both the Avestan Archives and the majority of Avestan scholars that could recite them after his conquest of the Persian Empire, however, Greek and Persian language texts do survive from before the time of Alexander that describe the ancient Archives. On the other hand, the Vedas have only been used in India throughout recorded history, and some do not believe they originate outside of Southern Asia. Nevertheless, a large amount of evidence has been amassed in the past century that show the ancient peoples of the Eurasian Steppes shared several elements with the society described in the Vedas, especially the oldest Vedas, and therefore the current view is that they were the people who composed these texts.

The question of which is older, the *Vedas* or the *Avesta*, has been debated by linguists and historians since the 1800s, with remarkably diverse views being proposed. The Vedas are generally dated by Indologists to no earlier than 1200 BC, the fabled 'beginning of the Iron-Age,' however, this view seems to be based on the European historians of the 1800s desire to have the Vedas be younger than the Torah, which was then believed to date to circa 1500 BC.

Today the *Torah* is dated to between 800 and 500 by most historians, and clearly, the *Vedas* are older than that. In point of fact, the older *Vedas* must date back to the Bronze Age, meaning before 1200 BC, and as they appear to have arrived in India by the onset of the Indian Iron Age, the older Vedas must predate 2400 BC.

On the other hand, the life of Zoroaster, who composed the earliest sections of the *Avesta*, traditionally dated to between 6300 and 6200 BC but Greek and Persian scholars before the time of Alexander the Great. Modern historians don't generally accept this dating either, and often place his life circa 550 BC, around the same time as the earliest references to him living before 6200 BC. Some scholars have even proposed later dates, meaning he would have lived a century or two after the oldest references to him. Obviously, there are problems with some of the dates proposed, however, scholars have a wide variety of views on this issue.

The Vedas

The *Vedas* are the oldest known collection of literature in India, however, their origin is widely disputed. The term *Vedas* is often misused by laymen as a catch-all for any ancient or even recent Hindu text that claims to be divinely inspired, however, it is, in fact, a specific group of four texts: the *Rig-veda, Sama-veda, Yajur-veda*, and *Atharva-veda*.[2] These four specific texts have been accepted as 'the *Vedas*' for thousands of years, however, at one point there were only three.[3] This is established by the references found in the *Rig-veda* to the 'three Vedas' found in the Taittiriya Brahmana (verse 3.12.9.1) and the Aitareya Brahmana (verse 5.32-33). Likewise early Buddhist Nikaya texts also only reference the 'three Vedas,' specifically omitting the *Atharva-veda*.[4] Historians generally agree that the *Atharva-veda* wasn't considered a Veda until after 500 BC, meaning, well into the Buddhist age when the Vedic religion was in decline.

Understanding the origin of this collection of texts is critical to understanding the history of the ancient Indo-Aryan peoples, and by extension their Iranian and European relatives, unfortunately, the subject is complex. To simplify the explanation of these various texts, the below graph is added showing the various dialects of Sanskrit, and the Vedic texts composed in them in roughly chronological order. This work will also simply the naming of the

[2]Gavin Flood (1996) *An Introduction to Hinduism*. Pages 35-39
[3]Frits Staal (2009) *Discovering the Vedas: Origins, Mantras, Rituals, Insights*. Pages 136-137
[4]Alex Wayman (1997) *Untying the Knots in Buddhism*. Pages 52-53

various texts, referring to various Brahmanas Aranyakas, and Upanishads by the Veda they are associated with, instead of their specific names, as there would be dozens of more names on the chart below if each individual text was named.

Each of the four Vedas is divided into four sections, the: *Samhita*, *Brahmana*, *Aranyaka*, and *Upanishads*, which means that there are sixteen major divisions within the four *Vedas*.[5] Additionally, there are sections of text that have been added later and are treated as separate sections by scholars. While all of these sections were composed in the Sanskrit language, they were not composed in the same dialect, and therefore a rough chronological order can be worked out.

The Samhita sections are collections of hymns and form the core of the four Vedas. Generally, when someone refers to a 'Veda' they are specifically referring to the Samhita section of the Veda. The Samhitas are the oldest section of each Veda, however, they are not composed in the same dialect, but rather four dialects. The *Rig-veda* Samhita is composed in two similar dialects, generally called Early-Rigvedic and Late-Rigvedic, while the *Sama-veda* Samhita is composed in Mantra Language, and the other two Samhitas are composed in a combination of Mantra Language and Samhita Prose.

---

[5]A Bhattacharya (2006) *Hindu Dharma: Introduction to Scriptures and Theology*. Pages 8-14

The *Rig-veda* is universally considered the oldest of the Vedas, and has been throughout recorded history. The *Rig-veda* Samhita itself is a collection of 1028 hymns, comprised of 10,600 verses, and organized into 10 books called mandalas. Mandalas 2 through 9 are in the oldest form of Sanskrit known, Early-Rigvedic, while mandalas 1 and 10 are later additions in Late-Rigvedic. The differences between the two Rigvedic dialects are less noticeable that the later language shifts, however, have been noted for centuries. The *Rig-veda* Samhita also includes a section of hymns known as the Khilani[6] that is recorded in Mantra Language Sanskrit, like the *Sama-veda* Samhita, and parts of the *Yajur-veda* and *Atharva-veda* Samhitas. It is generally accepted that these four texts were composed in Mantra Language, were composed around the same time, after the earlier Rigvedic texts of the *Rig-veda* Samhita.

The fact that *Yajur-veda* and *Atharva-veda* Samhitas are composed in two distinct dialects of Sanskrit is accepted as an indicator that the texts were likely composed over a long period of time, and while the Mantra Language core did not change, the later additions were fluid, changing with the language. It is worth noting that while these are referred to as texts today, they are not believed to have been written at the time, but rather sung as hymns or recited as mantras. Rigvedic was clearly a sung dialect, while Mantra Language was a spoken dialect intended for reciting mantras, which were generally spoken dur-

[6]Michael Witzel (1997) "The Development of the Vedic Canon and its Schools: The Social and Political Milieu," in *Inside the Texts, Beyond the Texts. New Approaches to the Study of the Vedas.* Pages 284-285

ing prayer, and then later Samhita Prose was a more poetic dialect, for public recitals.

The second sections in the Vedas are called the Brahmanas, which are theological treatises on the hymns of the Samhita sections. These sections are composed in a dialect called Brahmana Prose, which dates to after the sections composed in Mantra Language and Samhita Prose. This dialect was also used to compose the third and fourth sections of the *Rig-veda*, the: Aranyaka, and Upanishads, which leads to the conclusion that these sections of the *Rig-veda* were composed around the same time as the Brahmanas.

The Aranyakas are the third section of the Vedas, which are esoteric, while the Upanishads are the deeply spiritual treaties. For the past couple of centuries, the Upanishads have gained a great deal of esteem within Hinduism, and are currently considered a core of Hindu spiritual traditions by many Hindus. The Upanishads of the three later Vedas are all composed in Sutra Language Sanskrit, while the Aranyakas are composed in a mixture of Brahmana Prose and Sutra Language Sanskrit, implying the Aranyakas may date back to the same period as the Brahmanas, however, were later edited in the Sutra Language era.

THE VEDAS

Rigvedic	Mantra language	Samhita prose	Brahmana prose	Sutra language
Rig-veda Samhita				
	Rig-veda Khilani			
			Rig-Veda Brahmama	
			Rig-Veda Aranyaka	
			Rig-Veda Upanishads	
	Sama-veda Samhita			

THE VEDAS

Rigvedic	Mantra language	Samhita prose	Brahmana prose	Sutra language
Rig-veda Samhita				
			Sama-hita Brahmana	
			Sama-veda Aranyaka	
				Sama-veda Upanishads
	Yajur-veda Samhita			
			Yajur-veda Brahmanas	
			Yajur-veda Aranyaka	
				Yajur-veda Upanishads
	Atharva-veda Samhita			
			Atharva-veda Brahmana	
			Atharva-veda Aranyaka	
				Atharva-veda Upanishads

The Iron Ages

IRON AGES					
PERIOD	**METEORIC (CET)**	**METEORIC (ULT)**	**SMELTING (CET)**	**SMELTING (ULT)**	**COMMON USE**
Hattic (Turkey)			2500 BC	4000 BC	550 BC
Aïr Mt. (Niger)			2500 BC		1500 BC
Telengana (India)			2400 BC		600 BC
Haldummulla (Sri Lanka)			2400 BC		600 BC
Persia	5000 BC		2400 BC		550 BC
Lejja (Nigeria)			2400 BC		200 AD
Egypt	4000 BC	5800 BC	1500 BC		550 BC
Malhar (India)			1800 BC		300 BC
Yaz (Central Asia)			1500 BC		1300 BC
Sumer (Iraq)	4000 BC	5800 BC	1500 BC		550 BC
Akkad (Iraq)	2300 BC	3850 BC	1500 BC		550 BC
Assyria (Iraq-	1900 BC	3200 BC	1500 BC		550 BC

THE IRON AGES

<table>
<tr><td colspan="6" align="center">IRON AGES</td></tr>
<tr>
<td>PERIOD</td>
<td>METEORIC (CET)</td>
<td>METEORIC (ULT)</td>
<td>SMELTING (CET)</td>
<td>SMELTING (ULT)</td>
<td>COMMON USE</td>
</tr>
<tr><td>Syria)</td><td></td><td></td><td colspan="2"></td><td></td></tr>
<tr><td>Nok (Nigeria)</td><td></td><td></td><td colspan="2" align="center">1500 BC</td><td>200 AD</td></tr>
<tr><td>Termit (Niger)</td><td></td><td></td><td colspan="2" align="center">1500 BC</td><td>200 AD</td></tr>
<tr><td>Balkans</td><td></td><td></td><td colspan="2" align="center">1300 BC</td><td>550 BC</td></tr>
<tr><td>Greece</td><td></td><td></td><td colspan="2" align="center">1000 BC</td><td>500 BC</td></tr>
<tr><td>Nubia (Sudan)</td><td></td><td></td><td colspan="2" align="center">1000 BC</td><td>500 BC</td></tr>
<tr><td>Axum (Eritrea / Ethiopia)</td><td></td><td></td><td colspan="2" align="center">1000 BC</td><td>500 BC</td></tr>
<tr><td>Jordan</td><td></td><td></td><td colspan="2" align="center">930 BC</td><td>500 BC</td></tr>
<tr><td>China</td><td></td><td></td><td colspan="2" align="center">900 BC</td><td>100 BC</td></tr>
<tr><td>Roman Empire</td><td></td><td></td><td colspan="2" align="center">800 BC</td><td>100 AD</td></tr>
</table>

Unfortunately, knowing the order the Vedic texts were written in does not actually date the texts, and therefore various internal references are used to place the texts into specific cultures, which can then be used to date the texts themselves. These references are to specific metals and grains mentioned within the Vedas, specifically iron and rice. The earliest sections of the *Rig-veda* Samhita include mentions of metals (ayas) and therefore the entire collection must date to after the end of the stone age. The *Rig-veda* Samhita book 4 specifically refers to the gods smelting metal:

> *"...the gods smelting like metal ore the human generations..."(Rig-veda 4.2.17)*

The earliest mention of what is believed to be iron (krsna ayas / black metal) is found in the *Atharva-veda* Samhita[7] in the later Samhita Prose sections and the Shatapatha Brahmana in the *Yajur-veda*,[8] written in the Brahmana Prose. The mention of iron in this text is accepted as proof that the composition of this text took place after the onset of the Iron Age, however, the Iron Age began at different points in time across Eurasia. Meteoric iron had been used throughout the ancient world and was worth more than any other metal before the discovery of smelting. Iron artifacts have been found in the Iranian Plateau independently dated to 5000 BC,[9] as well as the pre-dynastic Badarian and Naqada cultures of Egypt and the Late Ubaid era of Iraq, both dated us-

---

[7]Dilip K. Chakrabarti (1992) *The Early use of Iron In India.*
[8]Constance Jones (2007) *Encyclopedia of Hinduism.* Page 404
[9]E. Photos (1989) "The Question of Meteoritic versus Smelted Nickel-Rich Iron: Archaeological Evidence and Experimental Results," in *World Archaeology.* 20 (3): 403–421.

ing the conventional dynastic timelines to circa 4000 BC CET/CMT[10] or 5800 BC using the Universal Long Timeline.

Several early iron-smelting sites have been found long preceding the general adoption of iron between 1200 and 550 BC, which is classically referred to as the Iron Age. The concept of the Iron Age dates back to the classic era Greeks, between 600 and 100 BC, who claimed the world had three historic eras, the stone age, the bronze age, and the iron age which they were in. The dating of the Iron Age is also based on their calculation, which held the Battle of Troy, circa 1200 BC, was at the end of the Bronze Age, and the conquest of the Iranian Plateau by the Persians took place after iron had become common.

Archaeological research in the 1800s brought this into doubt, as the Egyptians had some iron since the pre-dynastic era, and iron tools and weapons were found in small quantities throughout Egyptian history. The Egyptian word for iron was 'bi-a-n-pt' which translates as 'metal from the sky,' and is accepted as referring to any meteoric iron, however, the oldest known use of this word is from the 19th Dynasty, dated to between 1292 and 1189 BC CET (1322 to 1202 BC ULT). The word 'bi-a' was used since at least the Old Kingdom between 2686 and 2181 BC CET (4945 to 4003 BC ULT), where it appeared in the Pyramid Texts, however, it the word simply referred to any hard metal, and it appears that the Egyptians did not differentiate between hard metals at the time. Early Egyptologists concluded that all dynastic era iron was derived from meteors,

---

[10]R. F. Tylecote (1992) *A History of Metallurgy.* Page 3

and modern analysis generally agrees with this conclusion, as the surviving early Egyptian iron artifacts are high in nickel content, as iron-rich meteors generally are.

The development of iron smelting, which removes the impurities from the iron ore, was not significantly more advanced or complex than copper smelting, however, it does require a higher temperature. The melting point of copper is 1084° C (1984° F), while the melting point of iron is 1538°C (2500° F). The melting of copper was itself preceded by the smelting of tin and lead which both have temperatures low enough to be melted over a campfire, however copper requires a higher temperature and is believed to have first been smelted in ovens or pottery kilns. Iron smelting was a slightly more advanced technology than copper and tin smelting, as it includes adding coke or charcoal as a reducing agent.

The earliest known civilization to engage in iron-smelting was the Hattians of Central Anatolia circa 2500 BC CMT[11] (4000 BC ULT), who treated iron as a precious metal, like gold and silver. The Hittites that settled in the Hattian lands by 1664 BC CMT (3103 BC ULT) continued to use iron as a precious metal. The next oldest known site of iron smelting is in the Aïr Mountains of Niger, where iron smelting took place between 2500 and 1500 BC. These dates are established by carbon-dating, and not dynastic chronologies, and are therefore the same regardless of the timeline used. It isn't known for sure which culture was living in the Aïr Mountains at the time,

---

[11]Richard Cowen (April 1999) "Chapter 5: The Age of Iron," in *Essays on Geology, History, and People.*

however, the Hausa people were living in the Aïr Mountains before the Tureg were driven south by the Arabs in the 8th-century AD, and therefore assumed to be the descendants of the iron-working culture from 2500 to 1500 BC. Whichever culture it was, it appears to have developed iron smelting independently of an earlier culture, and likely inspired the development of iron-working in the Lejja culture in Nigeria circa 2000 BC.

The oldest known iron smelting on the Eurasian continent other than the Hattians and Hittites, is from between 2400 and 1800 BC, at several sites across the Indian states of Telangana, Karnataka, Andhra Pradesh, and Uttar Pradesh. The earliest iron artifacts are found in the southern states,[12] while the oldest slag deposits that prove large-scale iron production are found in Uttar Pradesh on the Gangetic plains in the north of India, dating to 1800 BC.[13] As iron is missing from the *Rig-veda* and the *Sama-veda*, but found in the *Yajur-veda* and *Atharva-veda* the implication is that the latter two were written after the onset of the Iron Age, while the earlier two predate it.

---

[12]Akinori Useugi, editor (2018) "Iron Age in South Asia," in *South Asian Archaeology,* Series 2

[13]Rakesh Tewari (2003) "The origins of Iron Working in India: New evidence from the Central Ganga plain and the Eastern Vindhyas," in *Antiquity.* 77 (297): 536–545.

Dating the Vedas

SANSKRIT (INDO-ARYAN) TIMELINE				
SANSKRIT DIALECT	**CULTURE (CIET)**	**TIMELINE (CIET)**	**CULTURE (ULT)**	**TIMELINE (ULT)**
Rigvedic	Early Vedic India	1800 (?) to 1100 BC	Cucuteni – Trypillia and Sredny Stog	4800 to 3000 BC
Mantra language			Maykop, Yamnaya, and Poltavka	3700 to 2100 BC
Samhita prose	Late Vedic India	1100 to 600 BC	Oxus (BMAC) and Early Iron Age India	2400 to 1800 BC
Brahmana prose			Early Vedic India	1800 to 1100 BC
Sutra language			Late Vedic India	1100 to 600 BC
Classical Sanskrit	Classical India	600 BC to 1300 AD	Classical India	600 BC to 1300 AD

The oldest specific mention of iron in the Vedas is accepted as being in the *Atharva-veda* Samhita, in the later Samhita Prose sections, and the next oldest mention of iron was in the *Yajur-veda* Brahmana, in Brahmana Prose. This would place the introduction of iron to the Vedic people, around the time that the Sanskrit language developed the Brahmana Prose. The *Atharva-veda* Samhita is also generally considered to have been composed in a different land than the earlier three Vedas, as it has a number of inconsistencies with the earlier Vedas. It is believed by some Indologists that this was the first Vedic text composed in India as the Indo-Aryan peoples migrated into India.

This would date the *Atharva-veda* Samhita to sometime between 2400 and 1600 BC. This date is not generally accepted, as the early Indologists of the Colonial era believed that the Iron Age in India must have taken place centuries after the Iron Age in the Middle East, instead of a thousand years earlier. Conventional Indo-European dating for the Vedic Texts would place the entire collection between 1200 and 600 BC, which is now proven to be quite impossible. Some more recent estimates by Indologists have moved the estimated dating to 1800 to 600 BC, however, any attempts to place the dating to an earlier period is hampered by the fact that the Indo-Aryan Mitanni invaded the Middle East circa 1500 BC CMT, and therefore the closely related Sanskrit texts must date to the same period. However, in the Universal Long Timeline, the Mitanni invasion of the Middle East dates to circa 2967 BC ULT, which allows the Vedic texts to have predated the Indian Iron Age, which we now know dates back to 2400 BC.

If the Samhita Prose sections of the Artharva-veda Samhita were written in Northern India between 2400 and 1800 BC, then the Samhita Prose sections of the *Yajur-veda* Samhita must date to the same time period, however, as it does not mention iron, it must have been composed outside of India. Given a number of lines of evidence, it is accepted that the Indo-Aryans migrated into India from Central Asia, carrying their Vedic Texts. A number of ancient Central Asian cultures have been proposed for the homeland of the Sanskrit speaking Indo-Aryans, including the Andronovo, Oxus, and Yaz cultures, as well as the ruins at Jeitun in Turkmenistan. Both the Andronovo and Yaz cultures are too late to be where the *Yajur-veda* Samhita was composed, and Jeitun was too early. The Oxus civilization, also called the Bactria-Margiana Archaeological Complex (BMAC), existed between 2400 and 1600 BC, at the same time as the development of iron smelting in India, and was, therefore, the most likely culture for the Samhita Prose Indo-Aryans to have started out, before migrating into India and coming into widespread contact with iron.

The Oxus civilization spanned the area of modern southern Turkmenistan, Uzbekistan, and Tajikistan, between 2400 and 1800 BC. Based on genetic analysis of the remains found in the civilization's cemeteries, there were a number of ethnic groups living in the area, including Middle Easterners (J*, J1, J2), Indo-Europeans (R1b, R2), Caucasians (G, T), Dravidians (L), and East Africans (E1b1a, E1b1b). The various Y-chromosome R haplogroups are generally associated with the Indo-European peoples and are the most common haplogroups found in Europe as well as Iran, Afghanistan, Pakistan, and northern India. Middle Easterners constitute the largest number of remains analyzed from the Oxus civilization, however, as the latter Vedic religion taught cremation, it is unlikely that many remains would be left from Sanskrit speaking peoples from that time period.

As the Samhita Prose sections of the Vedic Texts were the latter sections of the *Yajur-veda* and Artharva-veda Samhitas, the earlier Mantra Language sections must have been composed before the Indo-Aryans settled in the Oxus civilizations. As the civilization of the Rigvedic and Mantra Language sections of the Vedas describe a culture very much like the Kurgan culture of the Eurasian Steppes, it is generally accepted that the steppes could be the origin of the Indo-Aryan peoples, or their cultural ancestors. These cultural similarities include the use of horses and chariots, which are believed to originate on the steppes as the oldest remains of chariots have been found in the region. Additionally, horse burial sites have been found in the steppes that match the horse-sacrifice ceremonies found in the Rigveda Brahmana and *Yajur-veda* Samhita. These texts discussing horse burials are recorded in two dialects of Sanskrit, Samhita Prose and Brahmana Prose, which implies that the ancient Indo-Aryans were burying horses during the era they spoke these dialects, however, not during the earlier Rigvedic and Mantra Language eras, or later Sutra Language era.

Several closely related sites have been found across the steppes connected with the Kurgan cultures, including the Maykop, Yamnaya, Catacomb, and Poltavka cultures, spanning the era of 3700 and 2100 BC. The Maykop culture is often described as early Kurgan, although it was based farther south, in the Northern Caucasus region between 3700 and 3000 BC.[14] The Yamnaya culture is generally consid-

---

[14]Mariya Ivanova (2007) "The Chronology of the "Maikop Culture" in the North Caucasus: Changing Perspectives," in the *Ar-*

ered the height of the Kurgan culture, its name being
the Russian term meaning 'related to yama' (Ямная).
Yama (яма) is the Russian word 'pit,' which refers to
the burial pits under the mounds which are commonly called kurgans. The word Yama / Jama means
the same thing across the Slavic language family, appearing in all Slavic languages other than Polish. The
Yamnaya Culture spanned the region of Ukraine,
and southern and central Russia as far east as the
Urals between 3300 and 2600 BC. Yama is also the
name of the god of death and the underworld in the
Rigveda, meaning that the word has been in use in
the region for at least 5000 years.

The Yamnaya culture developed into the Catacomb culture in the west between 2900 and 2200 BC,
and the Poltavka culture in the east between 2800
and 2100 BC. The Catacomb culture developed in
Ukraine and southern Russia, while the Poltavka culture developed in the region between the Volga and
the Urals. Genetic analysis of remains from these
kurgan cultures shows that almost all remains had
the Y-DNA R haplogroups,[15] which are generally accepted as being Indo-European. Two Middle Eastern
(J*, J2a) males were also found in the region,[16] indicating long-distance trade with the Middle East existed by this time. One individual was also found be-

menian *Journal of Near Eastern Studies.* II: 7–39.
[15]W. Haak, et al. (2015) "Massive migration from the steppe was
a source for Indo-European languages in Europe," *Nature.* 522
(7555): 207–211.
[16]Eppie R. Jones, et al. (2015) "Upper Palaeolithic genomes re-
veal deep roots of modern Eurasians," in *Nature Communica-
tions.* 6: 8912.

long to haplogroup I2a2a1b1b,[17] which is generally found today in Northern Europe and Britain, and associated with lighter features, which implies that Mantra Language speakers were also trading with Northern Europe. Based on the analysis of the DNA recovered, it appears these people were similar in appearance to modern Iranians, with generally dark hair and eyes, and tan-colored to light brown skin.[18]

The Kurgan cultures developed from the earlier Cucuteni-Trypillia, and Sredny Stog cultures of Ukraine, Moldova, and Romania, between 4700 and 3500 BC. These cultures are widely accepted as the direct fore-bearers of the Maykop and Yamnaya cultures and have also been proposed as the potential homeland of the Indo-European people. Like the later kurgans, these cultures buried people in pits (яма / yama), however, they did not pile mounds above the pits. They also are believed to have been the first people that had domesticated horses.[19]

Genetic analysis has proven a connection between the Cucuteni-Trypillia culture and the Yamnaya culture, with peoples from western Ukraine, Moldova, and Romania migrating east into the traditional homeland of the Yamnaya culture circa 3600 BC.[20] The various remains that have been found

[17]Iain Mathieson (December 24, 2015) "Genome-wide patterns of selection in 230 ancient Eurasians," *Nature.* 528 (7583): 499–503

[18]Sandra Wilde (2014) "Direct evidence for positive selection of skin, hair, and eye pigmentation in Europeans during the last 5,000 y," in *PNAS.* 111 (13): 4832–4837.

[19]Rene J. Herrera (2018) *Ancestral DNA, Human Origins, and Migrations.* Page 518.

[20]Iain Mathieson, et al. (30 May 2017) *The Genomic History Of*

within the Cucuteni-Trypillia culture mostly belong to subclades of the Y-DNA R haplogroup, including R0, HV, and H. Individuals from the Middle Eastern J and T haplogroups have also been found, proving early contact between Eastern Europe and the Middle East by 6000 years ago. Given the common points between this culture and the culture of the *Rig-veda* Samhita, this is the most likely location of the composition of the *Rig-veda*. Mandala 1 of the *Rig-veda* mentioned chariots, which are proven to have been in use in Eastern Europe by 3500 BC.[21] Early wagons and chariots appeared near-simultaneously across Eastern Europe, Caucasia, and Mesopotamia at this time, however, are generally accepted to have originated in Ukraine, where horses are believed to have first been domesticated by the Sredny Stog culture.[22]

The later appearance of horse sacrifices in the Mantra Language texts connect this dialect conclusively with the kurgan cultures circa 3700 to 2100 BC, meaning the earlier Rigvedic texts had to date to an earlier culture, which the Cucuteni-Trypillia and Sredny Stog culture appears to be. Given the genetic migration from the Cucuteni-Trypillia culture east through the Sredny Stog culture to the later Yamnaya culture, the indication is that the Early-Rigvedic texts were likely composed in the Cucuteni-Trypillia culture between 4800 and 3500 BC,

Southeastern Europe
[21]David A. Anthony (2007) *The horse, the wheel, and language: how Bronze-Age riders from the Eurasian steppes shaped the modern world*
[22]Benjamin Fortson IV (2011) *Indo-European Language and Culture: An Introduction*, Second Edition.

while the Late-Rigvedic texts were likely composed in the Sredny Stog culture between 4500 and 3500 BC.

The Avesta

AVESTAN TIMELINE				
DIALECT	CULTURE (CIET)	TIMELINE (CIET)	CULTURE (ULT)	TIMELINE (ULT)
Old Avestan	Central Asia (?)	Before 1800 BC (?)	Bug - Dniester	6500 to 5500 BC
Younger Avestan			Samara, Dnieper - Donets, and Khvalynsk	5500 to 3500 BC
Youngest Avestan			Afanasievo	3700 to 2500 BC
Rigvedic	Early Vedic India	1800 (?) to 1100 BC	Cucuteni Trypillia and Sredny Stog	4800 to 3000 BC
Mantra language			Maykop, Yamnaya, and Poltavka	3700 to 2100 BC

The Vedic texts are the oldest Indo-Aryan texts, however, they aren't the oldest Indo-European texts. The Old Avestan texts are generally considered the oldest Indo-European texts, however, this is an issue that has been widely debated for thousands of years. The *Avesta* is the holy book of the ancient Zoroastrian religion, which was once the dominant religion of the Persian Empire. Like the Vedic texts, it is generally accepted that the *Avesta* was not written down until late in its existence, and was recited by a priesthood until the Achaemenian dynasty of Persia ordered the creation of an archive of Avestan texts near Persepolis circa 600 BC. This took place after the Persians had conquered the Iranian Plateau, and had adopted the cuneiform script from the Mesopotamians.

According to Zoroastrian records from later periods, there were approximately 30,000 Avestan texts in the archive, spanning the history of the Avestan-speaking peoples. This archive was burnt by Alexander the Great when he conquered the Persian Empire. He is also reported to have executed the priests who could recite the texts from memory. The surviving text known as the *Avesta* was compiled from surviving copies of Avestan texts the following decades, as Alexander's heirs did not share his disdain for the Persians, however, the vast majority of the text were lost forever. The *Avesta* itself is composed in an ancient Indo-Iranian language which is only known from one source, the *Avesta*. Like the Vedic Texts, the *Avesta* is composed in more than one dialect, either two or three depending on interpretation. The two established dialects of Avestan are called Old Avestan, and Younger Avestan. Additionally, some texts appear to be composed in a poor quality dialect, which is often described as an attempt by a non-Avestan speaker to compose in Avestan. This third dialect, if it is treated as one, is considered the Youngest Avestan, and in any event, the texts composed in it are considered the last sections of the surviving *Avesta* to have been composed.

The two established dialects are believed to have been both separated in time and location. This is based on the fact that not only does the dialect change, but the geographic names mentioned also change. Additionally, the Youngest Avestan texts, regardless of whether it is a dialect or not, were written in another distinct location as the geographic names change again. Old Avestan is also called Gathic Avestan, as it is the dialect that the Gathas were composed in. The Gathas are a collection of hymns attributed to the ancient philosopher and poet Zoroaster which served as the core of the Zoroastrian religion. The life of Zoroaster, also called Zarathustra, has also been a matter of debate for thousands of years. The earliest records of the life of Zoroaster universally agreed that he lived between 6200 and 6300 BC. This view was endorsed by all pre-Alexandrian scholars, including Xanthus and Hermippus in the 5th-century BC;[23] and Hermodorus, Eudoxus of Cnidus and Aristotle in the 4th-century BC.[24] All of these early scholars lived before the Avestan archives were destroyed by Alexander, and therefore they must have been basing this obscure date in the extreme past on what was recorded there.

This view changed in the Christian era, as early Christian 'historians' rewrote the history books of the world to make sure everything fits into the timeline described in the Septuagint, in which the world had been created circa 5500 BC. In the 3rd-century AD, Diogenes Laërtius placed the life is Zoroaster at approximately 1000 BC,[25] and in the 4th-century

[23]Martin Litchfield West (2013) *Hellenica: Volume III: Philosophy, Music and Metre*
[24]Michael Stausberg, et al. (2015) *The Wiley-Blackwell Companion to Zoroastrianism*
[25]Solomon Alexander Nigosian (1993) *The Zoroastrian Faith:*

Ammianus Marcellinus placed the life of Zoroaster around 550 BC. The later Islamic era Zoroastrian text called the Bundahishn appears to have used Ammianus Marcellinus as a source when it placed the life of Zoroaster circa 550 BC, a view which then became entrenched in Zoroastrianism.

Scholars in the past three centuries have repeated the views of all of the ancients, but generally date the life of Zoroaster sometime between 1700 and 500 BC. These dates are generally based on linguistic theories and are dated according to when the particular scholar believed the Avestan language developed in comparison to Sanskrit. Nevertheless, dating Zoroaster's life to circa 550 BC seems hopelessly illogical when the leading Greek scholars of the following century believed he had lived 5800 years earlier. Surely they would have known he had just recently lived and died.

The crux of the question of when Zoroaster lived, depended on two questions, when did Sanskrit develop, and when did Avestan develop in relation to Sanskrit. For those that believe that Sanskrit is older than Avestan, the life of Zoroaster could be any time before the Greeks mentioned his existence in the 5th-century. For those that believed that Avestan is older than Sanskrit, the life of Zoroaster must predate the composition of the *Rig-veda*. Unfortunately, the current school of Indology teaches that the *Rig-veda* was composed at the impossibly late date of circa 1500 to 1200 BC. This late date would allow Zoroaster to have lived as late at 1700 to 1500 BC.

Tradition and Modern Research

However, this late date is impossible based on the current knowledge of the earlier Iron Age in India.

The majority of linguists comparing Avestan to Sanskrit agree that the two languages were the most similar at the earliest phase, meaning that Early-Rigvedic was the closest Sanskrit dialect to Avestan. If the *Avesta* is divided by dialect, there are three sections, the Old and Younger Avestan sections, as well as the Vendidad, which is composed in the disputed Youngest Avestan dialect. A large body of commentary called the Zend is traditionally published with the *Avesta* written in Middle Persian, and dating to the Greek through early Islamic era when Zoroastrianism was the dominant religion in Persia.

In addition to Zoroaster's hymns which are known as the Gathas, the Yasna Haptanghaiti is composed in the Old Avestan dialect. The Yasna Haptanghaiti is a collection of seven chapters of prose verses that were inserted into the Gathas by early followers of Zoroaster. Linguists agree that these texts must have been written by people living shortly after the time of Zoroaster, and speaking the same language, however, the Yasna Haptanghaiti does form a distinctive form of Old Avestan, similar to the difference between the two dialects of Rigvedic.

The Younger Avestan sections of the *Avesta* comprise most of the text and are a distinctly different dialect from Old Avestan. This dialect is believed to have been spoken after Old Avestan was no longer being spoken, and is accepted as being spoken at a different geographic location based on the fact that the two texts do not contain the same geographic names. Some sections of these texts also seem to be pre-Zoroastrian, and my date back to an earlier Mithraic religion. Mithra was a major character in both the *Rig-veda* and *Avesta*, and it is believed by some scholars that there were converts to Zoroastrianism during the Younger Avestan era from the Mithraic religion. As virtually nothing is known of what that religion was, other scholars dismiss the claim. There was a major Mithraic cult in the Roman Empire that did not seem to be directly related to either the Vedic religion or Zoroastrianism, and therefore it could have been a descendant of the ancient Mithraic religion, however, this too is considered impossible to prove by most scholars.

The third dialect is found in the Vendidad, a historical text and legal code, somewhat akin to the Jewish Torah. The name means 'the law against the devas,' as the Zoroastrians considered the Vedic devas (gods) to be devils. Like Jews, Christians, and Muslims, the Zoroastrians were monotheists, in their case worshiping a god called Ahura Mazda, roughly translating a 'Great Wisdom.' Unfortunately, as so little of the Avestan archives survived Alexander's conquest, we cannot be sure if the language of the Vendidad constitutes a third dialect that many texts were written in or a fake text written during the Greek era. It is clear that the text does not use the same geographic names as the earlier Old and Younger Avestan texts, and most of the place-names appear on the Persian Plateau or in Central Asia. It is possible that this was an attempt to reconstruct an older text from fragments, or an outright fraud, however, it has never been treated as anything other than original Avestan text by Zoroastrians. If it is an original Avestan text, the implication is that there was a third dialect of Avestan, Youngest Avestan, and that this dialect was somewhere between Younger Avestan and an archaic form of Median or Persian. Avestan is generally considered closer to Scythian, a language spoken in ancient Afghanistan, Central Asia, and Southern Russia, and therefore classified as an East Iranian language, however, if Youngest Avestan is treated as a distinct dialect, then the West Iranian languages become children of Avestan, making Avestan the parent language of both the Eastern and Western branches of Iranian.

Regardless of whether Youngest Avestan was a dialect or not, the Old and Younger Avestan dialects appear to be older than the Rigvedic dialect of Sanskrit. This view is held by most linguists, however, some historians argue the issue. Among Hindus, the idea that Zoroaster existed before the Vedas is considered heretical, as he rejected the gods (devas), and many are motivated to date the *Avesta* to a later date for religious reasons. Nevertheless, there are several reasons why linguists agree that Avestan must predate Sanskrit. One of these reasons is due to the number of non-Indo-European loan words in Sanskrit, and which languages they derive from. As Sanskrit evolved, its speakers encountered several peoples that spoke different languages, and they learned new words, and grammatical structures from these other people, however, Avestan is a very 'pure' language, containing no known words of Uralic, Dravidian, or Munda origin. Sanskrit has loan words from all these language groups, and they can be detected entering the Sanskrit language as the language evolved through the various forms used to compose the Vedas.

The earliest known dialects of Sanskrit, Rigvedic, already had words in it that linguists believe originated in the Uralic languages to the northeast of the Cucuteni-Trypillia and Sredny Stog cultures. Little is known of the ancient Uralic cultures, however, they do appear to have been using metals from an early era, and their word for 'slave' was 'orya' which many linguists believe is derived from the word Arya, the name the Indo-Iranians called themselves. This implies that the Kurgan people were either selling their people as slaves, or the Uralics were raiding the Kurgan lands for slaves. The modern descendants of the Uralic peoples include the Hungarians, Finnish, and Estonians, along with several ethno-linguistic groups spread through the northern Russian Federation and Scandinavia, such as the Karelians, Sámi, Mansi, Khanty, Komi, Udmurtians, Mari, and Mordvins.

Linguists have been debating the relationship between the Uralic and Indo-European languages since the 1800s. The greater part of the Uralic languages' lexicon is shared by various Indo-European languages, however, it cannot be traced to a specific Indo-European group. Many of the borrowings can be traced to language groups found around the periphery of the Uralic lands including the Balto-Slavic, and Germanic language groups, however, some words are Indo-Iranian.[26] An example of the

---

[26]Johan Schalin (2009) *Lexicon of Early Indo-European Loan-*

borrowing from Indo-Iranian languages would be the word 'sata' which means 'hundred' in Sanskrit and Avestan, as well in Uralic languages.[27] Specific borrowings from Sanskrit into Uralic languages have also been noted such as the Finnish word for 'hammer:' 'vasara,' which is believed to be derived from the Sanskrit word 'vajra,' the name of Indra's hammer in the *Rig-veda*. The Sanskrit language also appears to have been modified by Uralic pronunciation, such as the shift from the Avestan *-tst- to the Sanskrit *-tt-. This Uralic inspired shift could only have happened in the northern steppes where the Sanskrit speaking Indo-Aryans would have encountered the Uralic speaking peoples of the Ural Mountains.

The Rigvedic dialect of Sanskrit was also missing the Dravidian loanwords that appeared in later Sanskrit dialects. The Dravidian languages are today indigenous to southern India, as well the highlands of Balochistan on the border of Pakistan and Iran, however, it is generally accepted by historians and Indologists that the ancient Indus Valley civilization was a Dravidian civilization. The era of the Indus Valley Civilization is also a matter of much debate, as its timeline was developed in the 1930s and correlated to the Conventional Mesopotamian Timeline, forcing the Bronze Age Indus Valley Civilization to be surrounded by the Iron Age Indian civilizations that are now known to have existed at the time. By comparing the Indus Valley Civilization to the timeline of Mesopotamia and Egypt on the Universal Long

---

words Preserved in Finnish
[27]David W. Anthony (2007) *The Horse, the Wheel, and Language.* Pages 371-411

Timeline using Indus seals found in Mesopotamia, it is now clear that the Indus Valley civilization existed much earlier, reaching its mature phase between 5000 and 3500 BC, and finally fading away by 2600 BC, before the rise of the Iron Age civilizations of India.

The Indus Valley Civilization traded extensively with the Sumerians during the Kish and Nippur dynasties, as well as the later Elamites and Akkadians. Common iconography has been found among the Indus, Sumerian, and Egyptian civilizations dating to the earliest periods of these three cultures. During the height of the Indus Civilization, they appear to have dominated most of South Asia and developed extensive trading networks as far north as Shortugai on the Oxus River of Central Asia. Oxus River is the ancient name of the Amu Darya River, which flowed north from Afghanistan to the Aral Sea. In ancient times the Great Aral Sea was massive, filling the modern desert regions of the Kyzyl Kum depression, being at least half the size of the Caspian Sea before it started shrinking around 3250 BC. The Indus trading port on the Oxus would have provided easy access to the Aral Sea at the time, and the Mantra Language Yamnaya and Poltavka cultures to the north.

The dominant grain eaten by the Indus people was rice, which first appeared in the Vedas in the Mantra Language *Yajur-veda* Samhita which had to have been composed on the Steppes by the Yamnaya and Poltavka cultures between 3700 and 2100 BC. This appears to be one of the first loan-words into the Sanskrit language, although a few others also appeared in the Mantra Language dialect, which indicates that the Steppes peoples must have begun trading with the Indus civilization. By the era of the Samhita Prose sections of the Vedas, Dravidian words begin to appear, although are few, however by the Brahmana Prose sections, they become more common. The later Sutra Language sections have so many Dravidian words, that it is generally agreed that the Sanskrit speaking peoples must have been permanently settled among Dravidian speaking peoples by the time these sections were composed.

Nevertheless, there appear to be no Dravidian or Uralic elements within the Avestan language, nor any reference to rice in the *Avesta*, supporting the conclusion that the Avestan language pre-dates the later Sanskrit language. The one argument often given for the late dating of the *Avesta* is that it does reference iron, called 'aysan,' however, this word is derived from the Avestan words meaning sky and stone, meaning the Avestans were referring to meteoric iron, and not smelted iron like the later Rigvedic 'krsna ayas.' It is also unclear if the Avestans were actually referring to iron, or if the word simply meant 'metal.' The lack of any Uralic or Dravidian elements within the debated Youngest Avestan dialect in the Vendidad supports the early composition of the texts, and by extension, the concept that it predated the later west and east Iranian dialects, nevertheless, as only one text survives in this language, linguists are unwilling to ascribe an entire culture to it, and generally settle on the idea that it was a later dialect or pseudo-dialect spoken by an impostor or in a remote culture that had become disconnected from the general advancement of the Indo-Iranian dialects.

As the Young Avestan dialect has to predate Rigvedic Sanskrit, regardless of the situation with Youngest Avestan, it must point to an even earlier civilization on the steppes, which is known from the archaeological record as a group of closely related cultures: the Samara, Dnieper-Donets, and Khvalynsk Cultures. Remains from these cultures belong to the same Y-DNA R haplogroup as the later Cucuteni-Trypillia and Sredny Stog cultures, proving the later kurgan cultures descended from these earlier cultures. The Samara culture was located on the Volga River near the city of Samara beginning around 5500 BC. The Samara culture developed into the Dnieper-Donets culture north of the Black Sea by 5000 BC, and the Khvalynsk culture in the Volga region by 4900 BC. The Khvalynsk culture of the Volga region continued until 3500 BC, while in Ukraine the Dnieper-Donets culture developed into the Early Rigvedic Cucuteni-Trypillia and Sredny Stog cultures between 4700 and 4200 BC.

These cultures used to bury their dead with the head of a horse, goat, or sheep, although it is unknown if the horses were domesticated or being hunted, however, it is generally accepted they were being eaten. A number of mass graves have been found which are interpreted as sites of human sacrifice, however, they could also be interpreted as burial sites of the remains from plagues or raids. Metals appear to have used as a sign of wealth, in these cultures, with tools and weapons still being made of flint. The metals used in this culture were imported from the more technologically advanced cultures of the Ural and Caucasian mountains, or melted from meteors, explaining the use of the word 'aysan' meaning 'sky stone.'

In addition to the western Cucuteni-Trypillia and Sredny Stog cultures, the Younger Avestan cultures also gave rise to the Afanasievo culture to the east. The Afanasievo culture occupied southern Siberia, eastern Kazakhstan, and western Mongolia between 3300 and 2500 BC, and were both culturally and genetically descended from the Dnieper-Donets and Khvalynsk cultures. Like the earlier cultures, the Afanasievo continued to use flint tools, and the only known metals found in their graves were jewelry imported from other lands. Their existence runs parallel to the early bronze age Rigvedic culture in the western Steppes, and therefore they could not be trading greatly with the early Sanskrit speakers, as they did not import metalworking processes from them. Depending on one's view of the Youngest Avestan language debate, this culture could either be seen as the Youngest Avestan speaking people or Proto-Scythians. In either event, the Scythians would later rise in the region, speaking a language that linguists agree is the most like Avestan of the languages still spoken in the classic era of Greco-Roman civilization.

Linguists also agree that the Old Avestan speakers lived earlier than the Younger Avestan speakers, and in a different region. The precursor to the Samara and Dnieper-Donets cultures is generally regarded as being Bug-Dniester culture, in the chernozem region of Moldova and Ukraine between 6500 and 5500 BC. The people of the Bug-Dniester culture are believed to have settled in the region from the Volga region, after crossing Siberia from the Lake Baikal region. The idea that these people originated originally in the Lake Baikal region of Siberia is based on the pottery style that originated there spreading across the Steppes to the chernozem region. This concept is supported by genetic research into remains discovered in the Baikal region that show the population there around 24,000 years ago belonged to the Y-DNA R* haplogroup, the ancestral group of most Europeans and South Asians. Additional studies have found the R haplogroup subclades in the remains at Afontova Gora, in southwest Siberia circa 18,000 years ago, and the subsequently in then later in the remains of the various steppes cultures before they spread out throughout Eurasia. The Bug-Dniester culture is the earliest culture associated with the Indo-European peoples that are believed to have been a farming society, cultivating einkorn, emmer, and spelt, as well as raising cattle.[28]

As the Bug-Dniester culture appears to be the latest culture that the Old Avestan speaking people could have resided in and that they would have been there between 6500 and 5500 BC, the life of Zoroaster may well have been between 6300 and 6200 BC as the ancient scholars claimed. The society of Zoroaster was clearly described as being very primitive, and his teaching appears to have had little impact on the overall culture. Both the Younger Avestan sections of the *Avesta* and the Vendidad de-

[28]David W. Anthony (2007) *The Horse, the Wheel, and Language.* Pages 140, 147-151

scribe the followers of Zoroaster surrounded by heathens, implying the religion did not become widespread until the Achaemenian dynasty when it became the state religion of the Persian Empire. The majority of the Avestan speaking peoples appear to have been following the Vedic religion, and before that pre-Vedic cults. The name of the Zoroastrian God confirms this, as Ahura Mazda, includes the word Ahura, the Avestan version of Asura, the ancient gods of the early-Vedic era. Indra, Rudra, Varuna, and several ancient Vedic gods were called Asuras in the *Rig-veda*, however, this term fell out of use, and today they are considered devas (gods) by Hindus, while Asuras are seen as ancient demons or evil gods.

The Old Avestan Bug-Dniester culture appears to have been extremely successful, and the Y-DNA R haplogroup subclades spread from there back across the steppes and into Asia, creating several new cultures as it went. The oldest known remains belonging to the R* haplogroup are approximately 24,000 years old and were found in the Baikal region of Siberia. Based on the rest of the genome it is known that the boy had tan-colored skin, brown eyes, black hair, and Mongolian-type physiology. All early remains containing R haplogroup subclades have similar features until approximately 14,700 years ago when blond hair and lighter eye shades begin to appear in the genome of the remains.[29] These lighter tones were most likely a result of interbreeding with Uralic peoples encountered as the R haplogroup peo-

---

[29]I. Mathieson (2018) "The Genomic History Of Southeastern Europe," *Nature*. 555: 197-203.

ples moved west from Siberia, and may have also been present in the indigenous population in Eastern Europe when they arrived. The Avestan language most-likely developed within the Bug-Dniester region, as there would have already been several Indo-European languages in the region when the R haplogroup people settled in the area. The almost artificial seeming specific and precise rules of Old Avestan point to a language adopted by an immigrant population that adapted the linguistic rules they already knew and applied them to a new language.

The Greco-Aryans

GRECO-ARYAN TIMELINE				
LANGUAGE GROUP	CULTURE (CIET)	TIMELINE (CIET)	CULTURE (ULT)	TIMELINE (ULT)
Greco - Aryan	Eastern Europe (?)	Before 1800 BC (?)	Iron Gates Mesolithic	11,000 to 3500 BC
Greco - Armenian	Eastern Europe (?)	Before 1800 BC (?)	Starčevo - Körös - Criş	6200 to 5300 BC
Paleo - Balkan	Balkan Peninsula	Before 1800 BC (?)	Turdaş - Vinča	5700 to 4500 BC
Proto - Greek	Balkan Peninsula	Before 3200 BC	Gumelniţa - Kodžader- men - Karanovo	4700 to 3950 BC
Helladic Greek	Greece	3200 to 1050 BC	Greece	3200 to 1050 BC
Mycenaean Greek	Greece	1600 to 1100 BC	Greece	1600 to 1100 BC

Old Avestan was not the earliest Indo-European language and must have been in the general vicinity of several other Indo-European languages, all spoken by non-Y-DNA R haplogroup people. The exact evolution of the various Indo-European language groups is a matter of great debate among linguists, however, most agree that there was a Proto-Indo-Iranian or Greco-Aryan or Indo-Slavic language that would have preceded Old Avestan. This language group would have been the mother language of the various Indo-Aryan, Iranian, Armenian, Greek, and Albanian languages. This Greco-Aryan language could not have been spoken by a steppes culture as they would have carried the Y-DNA R haplogroup at an earlier point if they were from the steppes.

Archaeological evidence shows a great deal contact between the Bug-Dniester culture and the cultures of the Danube River and the Carpathian Mountains, especially the Starčevo-Kőrös-Criş culture between 6200 and 5300 BC. This culture was not an R haplogroup people, instead of being composed of H and G Y-DNA haplogroups. These haplogroups are commonly found today in the Dravidians of southern India, and peoples of the Caucasus Mountains and northwest Iran. These haplogroups are believed to have been common in the indigenous peoples of southern Europe before the R haplogroup became dominant. The ancestral culture of the Starčevo-Kőrös-Criş culture is believed to be the Iron Gates Mesolithic culture which was based in the Danube region since 11,000 BC.

Given the long contact between these cultures and the Bug-Dniester culture, these cultures must have been Indo-European speaking, and the earlier Iron Gates culture must have been the source of the Greco-Aryan language which the haplogroup R peoples adopted. The Iron Gates Mesolithic culture existed in the region of Iron Gates where the Danube River crosses from Serbia into Romania. It includes the ruins of Lepenski Vir, nicknamed 'the first city in Europe.'[30] Lepenski Vir was a stone-age town with at least ten satellite villages that existed between 6300 and 6000 BC. While Lepenski Vir may have been the

---

[30]Hristivoje Pavlović (23 August 2007) "Tajne Lepenskog Vira IV - Zapanjujuća veština obrade kamena," in *Politika*

peak of the culture, similar artifacts in the region go back to at least 11,000 BC, indicating an extremely long period of habitation. While it is the most likely location of the Greco-Aryan speaking people, it would have been quite different from the later steppes cultures, as it was a river-based culture instead of a culture that traveled by horseback. The Danube River would have given them access not only to the chernozem region where the Bug-Dniester culture was located, but also deep into the European continent, as today it passes through, or serves as a border to Germany, Austria, Slovakia, Hungary, Croatia, Serbia, Bulgaria, Romania, and Ukraine, before finding its way to the Black Sea.

If the Greco-Aryan language was the language of the Iron Gates culture, then the origin of the Indo-European languages would date back to the Magdalenian cultures of Europe, between 17,000 and 12,000 years ago. These cultures roamed across the European continent hunting the game that spread into the region as the glaciers retreated. Their ancestors are believed to have mainly been from the Caucasus and Anatolia. A significant number of stone tools and weapons have been found across Europe that bear a striking resemblance and the production of tools is believed to have been fairly standardized, implying a common culture. This culture seems to have formed into a northern culture focused on the then massive Lake Ancylus that filled the Baltic Sea, and a southern culture that existed in the Balkans along the Danube River. The northern culture was likely the origin of the other surviving branch of the

Indo-European languages, the West-European languages.

The Starčevo-Kőrös-Criş culture emerged from the Iron Gates culture along the Danube and a tributary river called the Kőrös Hungarian and Criş in Romanian, roughly contemporaneously with the Old-Avestan culture in the Bug-Dniester region. This culture covered a sizable area in the Balkan peninsula, including regions of the modern states of Serbia, Montenegro, Bosnia-Herzegovina, Bulgaria, Croatia, Hungary, Macedonia, and Romania. Like the earlier Iron Gates culture, it appears to have been a principally river-going stone-aged culture and based on similarities between the Indo-Iranian languages and the Greco-Armenian languages the Starčevo-Kőrös-Criş culture likely spoke the Greco-Armenian language. The Greco-Armenian language is a theoretical language that the Greek, Armenian, and Albanian languages descend from. This theoretical language is not universally accepted, however, these three language groups do have significant similarities indicating a common region of origin with significant prolonged contact and borrowing between the languages, and therefore even if the Greco-Armenian language did not exist, the Starčevo-Kőrös-Criş culture is the most likely region where these languages originate.

This same region was later home to the Turdaş-Vinča culture between 5700 and 4500 BC, which seems to have developed directly from the earlier Greco-Armenian culture in the area. Based on the linguistic analysis the Armenian branch of this language group must have split off by then, and it is possible that they were either living in the steppes among the Sanskrit speakers or had already migrated to the northern Caucasus region. The Turdaş-Vinča culture was in both the right time and place to be the locus of the Paleo-Balkan culture, which was the ancestral mother culture of the Greek and Albanian language groups. Paleo-Balkan is also a disputed proto-language, however, it is generally more accepted than Greco-Armenian, as there are a large number of similarities between Greek and Albanian that are difficult to explain from cultural borrowing.

The Turdaş-Vinča culture is generally considered one of the earliest cultures to use a form of writing by advocates of the conventional timelines, as this culture is dated based on scientific evidence to between 5700 and 4500 BC when the conventional timelines claim Egypt and Sumer did not even exist. When viewed on the Universal Long Timeline, all three cultures, along with the Indus Civilization in South Asia developed writing systems around the same time as the Turdaş-Vinča culture in the Balkans. The Danube script itself is highly debated as only short phrases have been found using the script, generally scratched into small coin-like tokens. These tokens are not dissimilar to the tokens used in the Ubaid and Uruk periods of Mesopotamian Archaeology, which are dated to between 6500 and 3100 BC CMT (8331 to 4931 BC ULT). In the case of the Mesopotamians, the symbols of the tokens are later found in the early pictographic script of the Jemdet Nasr and Early Dynastic eras between 3100 and 2334 BC CMT (4931 to 3555 BC ULT), which proves the symbols were used for writing.

Unfortunately, there are no longer known works from the Balkans that prove this text was used for writing more than names or simple terms like cow or fish. Of the 5421 artifacts found inscribed with this script, only 1178 have more than one symbol.[31] Almost all of these symbols, that aren't on the tokens are carved into pottery, implying they may have been names of the artisans that created the work. If this is the case, it implies either a literate society in which everyone could read the symbols or, a non-literate society in which the symbols were merely a primitive trade-mark system. The symbols themselves are abstract, unlike the pictographic symbols used in early Sumer, the hieroglyphs of Egypt, and the Indus Valley Script. This implies a script that had been in use for a long enough time that the symbols had evolved from their original form which was likely pictures of animals and objects. The development of more iconic scripts from simple pictures is well established in Egypt, Mesopotamia, South Asia, China, and Mexico, where indigenous scripts all evolved from pictures, and therefore, it seems highly probable that this script was a later development of a script recorded on a medium that is now lost to time, such as parchment or vellum. An alternate interpretation for these tokens with unique symbols of them is that they were being used as seals, which would imply a form of parchment that could be rolled and sealed with wax, like in Mesopotamia and the Indus Valley Civilization.

---

[31]Marco Merlini (2009) *Introduction to the Danube script*

Like the Sanskrit speakers on the steppes at the time, the Paleo-Balkans seem to have only used metal for jewelry and continued to use flint tools, although, unlike the Sanskrit speakers, they were working copper mines to produce the jewelry themselves. This culture gave rise to several smaller cultures in the western Balkans, as well as the Gumelniţa-Karanovo culture spanning much of modern Bulgaria and Romania between 4700 and 3950 BC. Like the earlier Paleo-Balkan culture in the Turdaş-Vinča region, the Gumelniţa-Karanovo culture continued to use the Danube script, which by the end of their civilization was in use for at least a thousand years.

Like the smaller west Balkans cultures, the Gumelniţa-Karanovo culture seems to have collapsed by 4000 BC, although no signs of conquest and resettlement have been found. At this point, the Kurgan culture was thriving on the steppes, and the Sanskrit speakers likely introduced the horse to the Balkans at this time, which would have allowed the people to spread out farther from the rivers, likely fragmenting the culture that had been living along the rivers of Bulgaria and Romania into several closely related tribes over the next millennium. Given the location of the Gumelniţa-Karanovo culture, it seems highly probable that this was the Proto-Greek culture, which is generally accepted as having been somewhere in the Balkans at the time.

Farther south in Greece, another culture had been developing since 7510 BC referred to as the Sesklo or Neolithic Greece culture. This culture is generally accepted as having not been a Greek culture, however, some Greek nationalists would like to draft it into the Greek pre-history. The primary reason why historians have traditionally claimed the Greeks migrated south into Greece from the Balkans is due to the fact that the Greeks themselves recorded this as their ancient place of origin. This migration into Greece took place sometime before the battle of Troy, as the Greeks had settled in Greece and built cities by that time.

The Sesklo culture itself was related to the cultures farther north in the Balkans at an early point, and similarities have been found between pre-Sesklo artifacts and Iron Gates artifacts. This implies an early off-shoot culture that traveled south, likely by boat, and settled in Greece by 7510 BC. This culture seems to have developed generally isolated from the cultures of the Balkans, however, would have been impacted by the spread of horses after 4000 BC. The Selko culture disappeared around 3200 BC, implying the people had left Greece for some reason. This time period is shortly after the Great Shock of 3250 BC, a time period when the world's climate changed significantly into a neo-glacial period that lasted until around 1500 BC.

There are several pieces of evidence supporting the existence of this Great Shock of 3250 BC. During this time the world's weather became stormier, and there was far more rain, which would have caused significant storms in the Aegean Sea, and significant flooding along rivers and swamps throughout the world.[32] The GISP2 ice core samples from Greenland

---

[32]Lisa L. Ely, et al. (October 15, 1993) "A 5000-Year Record of Extreme Floods and Climate Change in the Southwestern

show there was a spike in atmospheric sulfate at 3250 BC, believed to have been from an increasing number of polynyas in the Arctic, caused by an expansion of oceanic surface ice.[33] The GRIP ice core sample from Greenland shows the 3250 BC point as being at a low point in atmospheric methane, followed by a rapid increase over the next 200 years, which is attributed to an abrupt increase in global wetlands.[34] Additionally, the ice core samples from the Huascaran glacier in Peru, show an abrupt cooling at about 3250 BC.[35]

The disappearance of the Sesklo culture from Greece mirrors the appearance of the Hittite culture in Anatolia, and given the stormy weather at the time, it is probable that the Sesklo culture transitioned from being a primarily maritime culture to a horseback culture around this time. The fragmented and mountainous nature of Greece would have been far less appealing than the open spaces of Anatolia, although the reason for their movement was more likely to find food, as they would have been depending on the sea as a source of food until that time. Akkadian records from the time mention the Hittites progressively conquering the Hattian culture over the next century, and ultimately established their Old Kingdom circa 3103 BC ULT (1664 BC CMT).

United States," *Science*, New Series, Volume 262, Number 5132, Pages 410-412

[33]G. A. Zielinski, et al. (1994) *Nature*, Volume 264, Page 948

[34]T. Blunier, et al. (1995) *Nature*, Volume 374, Page 47

[35]L. G. Thompson, et al. (July 7, 1995) "Late Glacial Stage and Holocene Tropical IceCore Records from Huascaran, Peru," *Science*, Volume 269, Pages 46-50

This would naturally lead to the conclusion that the Sesklo culture was a proto-Hittite culture. The Hittites are well established as one of the early off-shoots of the Indo-European culture, however, their language is so different from the other Indo-European languages that they must have developed in isolation for several millennia before invading Anatolia. This is a significant problem for the supporters of the conventional timelines, as there is no time for Hittite to develop. The conventional timeline of Indo-European linguistics is itself a matter of great debate, with different researchers placing the origin of the Indo-European culture anywhere between 5500 and 1800 BC. Most linguists point to the earlier periods, as Indo-European languages have gone through several shifts throughout their existence. Tracing the changes in Indo-Iranian languages, which is possible thanks to the existence of the *Avesta* and Vedas, we see no less than eight distinct linguistic eras before the emergence of Classical Sanskrit and Old Persian circa 600 BC. Before this, there had to have been several linguistic eras, which had to at least include a Greco-Aryan (or Indo-Slavic) and Indo-European era, although most linguists would place more eras between the emergence of Old Avestan and Rigvedic Sanskrit from the Proto-Indo-European language.

To resolve this lack of time in the conventional timelines, some linguists have proposed an Indo-Anatolian language that preceded the Indo-European languages, as this would have allowed enough time for the Hittite language to deviate so far from the other Indo-European languages. However, when viewing the development of these cultures and languages on the Universal Line Timeline, it becomes clear that Hittite could have developed long after the Proto-Indo-European, in relative isolation from the other Indo-Europeans to the north. Little can be known for certain of the original Hittite homeland, other than the likelihood that it was a mountainous land, as their name for themselves was the Nesi, which is believed to be derived from the word 'mountain.'

After the Hittites left Greece, the Greeks began settling the region. The earliest artifacts attributed to Greeks date to around 3200 BC and are referred to Helladic, or early Greek. These artifacts begin to appear at the same time the Sesklo people disappear, however, there are no signs of massacres, and it appears the Greeks simply expanded down into the vacated lands. It is likely that not all the Sesklo left Greece, however, those that stayed behind were assimilated into Greek culture by the Mycenaean era, between 1600 and 1100 BC. The Proto-Greeks in the Balkans were likely dislodged by flooding rivers during the Great Shock of 3250 BC, which would have led to migrations into mountainous territory, however, this was also a period of rapid cooling, which would have driven the Proto-Greeks south. In any event, according to their records, not all Greek tribes moved south at that time, as the Dorians were later recorded as having migrated into Greece after the collapse at the end of the Mycenaean era, circa 1100 BC.

The Mycenaean Greeks were the first Greeks that are known to have used a written script, the Linear-

B script, that they appear to have adopted from the Minoans. Linear-A is the still undeciphered Minoan version of the script, which was used alongside Minoan Hieroglyphs. The earliest surviving Linear-B inscriptions are dated to circa 1450 BC and provide the earliest glimpse into the Greek minds of the time. At that time the Greeks were worshiping some of the same gods as their classical era descendants, including Poseidon, Dionysus, Persephone, and Hades. Some of these names have also been found in Linear-A, however, while the sounds of the symbols are believed to be the same as the sounds used by the Greeks, the language itself is undeciphered.

The West-Europeans

WEST-EUROPEAN TIMELINE				
LANGUAGE GROUP	CULTURE (CIET)	TIMELINE (CIET)	CULTURE (ULT)	TIMELINE (ULT)
Proto - West - European			Ahrensburg	12,900 to 11,700 BC
West - European			Swiderian	11,000 to 8200 BC
Late - West - European			Magle-mosian	9000 to 6000 BC
Italo - Celtic	Baden and/or Beaker culture	4300 to 1800 BC	Baden and/or Beaker culture	4300 to 1800 BC
Proto - Germanic	Nordic bronze age	1700 to 500 BC	Funnel-beaker, Globular Amphora, and Corded Ware	3200 to 1060 BC
Celtic	Atlantic bronze age	1700 to 700 BC	Atlantic bronze age	1700 to 700 BC
Proto - Nordic	Viking era	800 to 1100 AD	Nordic bronze age	1700 to 500 BC

As the last possible culture that could have been the Old Avestan culture appears to have been the Bug-Dniester Culture of 6500 to 5500 BC, making their Greco-Aryan ancestral culture likely the Iron Gates culture in the Danube between 11,000 and 6000 BC, the other surviving branch of the Indo-European languages, the West-European languages, had to be around at the same time. The West-European languages include the Germanic, Italic, and Celtic languages, which all share certain common elements. The existence of a proto-Italo-Celtic language has long been accepted by some linguists, while others argue that the Celtic languages are an offshoot of Proto-Italic, or that the Italic languages are an offshoot of Proto-Celtic. This debate seems to be somewhat arbitrary, and no-doubt influenced by nationalism to an extent. In any event. there was a common Italo-Celtic language at one point, regardless of how it is classified.

The inclusion of Germanic with Italo-Celtic is more contentious, as the Germanic languages also share a great deal with the Balto-Slavic languages, however, the Germanic and Balto-Slavic similarities can be attributed to later contact during the formative period of the Balto-Slavic languages, which is generally dated to around the time of the Greco-Roman cultures of the classic era. The similarities between Germanic and Italo-Celtic cannot be dismissed as late developments as all of these language groups long precede the classical era. 11,000 years ago, there was another significant stone-aged culture in Europe besides the Iron Gates Culture, the Swiderian culture of modern Poland and Lithuania. The Swiderians were also a river-going people, who used the rivers emptying into the Baltic sea as highways across Eastern Europe the same way the Vikings would thousands of years later.

This culture had similar technology to the Iron Gate culture on the Danube but appears to have been less artistic, and most likely had a harder time surviving in the climate of Eastern Europe than the Greco-Aryans had on the Danube. This culture was descended from the Ahrensburg culture, who inhabited northern Germany through southern England between 12,900 and 11,700 BC, and was in turn a descendant of the Magdalenian cultures that migrated into Europe between 17,000 and 12,000 years ago. The Ahrensburg culture appears to have moved east into the more sheltered region of the Baltic from the more exposed region of the North Sea, although the exact reason is unknown, it was likely due to climatic shifts. The Baltic was at the time an ice lake formed from melting glaciers which persisted until approximately 8300 BC when it was exposed to the sea and became a brackish sea archeoclimatologists call the Yoldia Sea.[36]

This transition from ice lake to brackish sea circa 8300 BC seems to have led to the end of the Swiderian culture, as within a century the culture disappears from the archaeological record. An offshoot culture called the Maglemosian culture formed around the coasts of Baltic ice lake beginning around 9000 BC, which seems to have thrived as the Baltic ice lake warms and became the brackish Yoldia Sea, and they continue along the shores of the Yoldia until approximately 6000 BC. During this time the Yoldia Sea became isolated from the North sea again, forming a massive freshwater lake called Ancylus Lake by archeoclimatologists. This transition does not seem to have affected the Maglemosian culture

---

[36]Nils-Axel Mörner (1995) "The Baltic Ice Lake-Yoldia Sea transition," in *Quaternary International.* 27: 95–98.

in the region, however, the subsequent draining of the Ancylus when the lake reconnected to the North Sea seems to have destroyed the civilization. Ancylus Lake was significantly higher than the sea-level of the ocean, covering large low-lying sections of modern Sweden, Finland, and Estonia, which rapidly drained around 6000 BC when the lake reconnected to the North Sea, and the Maglemosian culture disappeared at the same time.

Assuming this was the original West-European speaking homeland, then the Funnelbeaker culture of Poland, Denmark, Northern Germany, and Southern Sweden between 4300 and 2800 BC would no doubt be a northern descendant of West-Europeans, and likely the Proto-Germanic culture. The Baden culture to the south, in the lands of Hungary, Czechia, Austria, and Slovakia between 3600 and 2800 BC is occasionally proposed as the original homeland of the Italo-Celts by proponents of that proto-language, and therefore could easily be a southern branch of West-European peoples that migrated back into the Danube area.

In the north, the Funnelbeaker culture developed into the Globular Amphora culture between 3400 and 2800 BC, and then the Corded Ware culture between 2900 and 2350 BC. This last culture encompassed all of the lands east of the Rhine that the Romans traditionally attributed to the Germans, but also expanded northeast through Poland and the Baltic into Finland and north-western Russia. Likely, some of this culture was not Proto-Germanic, however, it is plausible that Proto-Germanic was used as a common language of trade and politics across the region, which would explain the Germanic words in Uralic languages, as well as the common elements of between Germanic and Balto-Slavic languages, assuming the Balto-Slavs were a northern offshoot of the Greco-Aryans or Sanskrit speakers that fell under the Germanic sphere at that time.

To the south and west, the Baden culture seems to have evolved into, or been drawn into the Bell Beaker Culture, which is often associated with the spread of the Celtic or Italo-Celtic culture. The Bell Beaker Culture spread from the northern Danube out across Western Europe between 4300 and 1800 BC, and at its peak encompassed most of France, Spain, Portugal, and Britain, as well as parts of Italy. In the west, this culture was later replaced by the Atlantic Bronze Age between 1300 and 700 BC, which may have been spread by the Proto-Celtic language. Proto-Celtic is generally accepted as having been a creole of various old languages in western Europe that was used as a trade language. It is likely the Celts never spoke a common language, but a spectrum of similar languages influenced by Proto-Italo-Celtic.

The Balto-Slavs

BALTO-SLAVIC TIMELINE				
LANGUAGE GROUP	**CULTURE (CIET)**	**TIMELINE (CIET)**	**CULTURE (ULT)**	**TIMELINE (ULT)**
Greo-Aryan	Eastern Europe (?)	Before 1800 BC (?)	Iron Gates Mesolitic	11,000 to 3500 BC
Rigvedic	Early Vedic India	1800 (?) to 1100 BC	Cucuteni – Trypillia and Sredny Stog	4800 to 3000 BC
Mantra language			Maykop, Yamnaya, and Poltavka	3700 to 2100 BC
Proto - Germanic	Nordic bronze age	1700 to 500 BC	Funnel-beaker, Globular Amphora, and Corded Ware	3200 to 1060 BC
Proto - Balto - Slavic	Eastern Europe	Before 1500 BC (?)	Trzciniec - Komariv	1900 to 1200 BC
Balto - Slavic	Eastern Europe	Before 1500 BC (?)	Lusatian	1300 to 500 BC
Proto - Slavic	Eastern Europe	500 to 900 AD	Pomeranian	650 to 150 BC
West - Slavic	Eastern Europe	700 to 1400 AD	Oksywie - Wielbark	200 BC to 400 AD
East - Slavic	Eastern Europe	800 to 1200 AD	Przeworsk	300 BC to 500 AD

The development of the Balto-Slavic language group in north-central Europe is another highly debated issue. Some linguists believed the language group did not even exist, instead claiming the two language groups merely co-existed in the same region. In either case, the Baltic and Slavic languages share a great deal, and both appear to be an offshoot of either Sanskrit or Greco-Aryan, and then influenced by Proto-Germanic.

If the Balto-Slavic language did exist, it creates another problem for the Conventional Indo-European Timeline, as linguists have stated it could not have existed more recently that around 3000 to 3500 years ago, meaning that it existed at the same time as Sanskrit, which is should be a descended of. This issue is sidestepped if one dismissed the Balto-Slavic language and simply claims that they are very similar languages, that developed in the same region, from the same proto-language, say Greco-Aryan, and were then influenced by the same foreign languages, such as Proto-Germanic, however, one then needs to explain the large number of identical words and concepts shared in the Balto-Slavic languages and Sanskrit, yet not shared by Avestan.

The division of the Slavic languages into the Eastern, Southern, and Western Slavic language groups is another debated issue, as the Conventional Indo-European Timeline requires all of this to have happened in the Middle Ages. This means that in the Conventional Indo-European Timeline there were no Poles or Czechs or Bulgarians, or Serbo-Croats until after the year 500 AD, and no Russians or Ukrainians until around the year 900 AD. This determination is based on the fact that the Slavs were mostly illiterate until 900 AD, and the writing that does remain from the time period is all in Old Slavonic, the script developed in Bulgaria and Serbia at that time. Old Slavonic was used by Slavs throughout Greek-influenced lands, while the Roman-influenced German and Celtic lands adopted the Latin alphabet.

This concept that the Slavs did not begin to separate into differentiated language groups until after the year 500 AD is required in the Conventional Indo-European Timeline as there is no time for them to have separated earlier. Unfortunately, it contradicts all logic. In order for a non-literate people to maintain a common-dialect, they would all need to live in a common area, which in the Conventional Indo-European Timeline is modern Poland. After 500 AD, they began to rapidly breed and cover Eastern Europe, expanding south to Bulgaria and Serbia almost instantly, where they came into contact with the Greeks and developed the Old Slavonic alphabet, but did not bother teaching it to the relatives back in Poland, who they broke off all contact with. Then the Old Slavonic-using Bulgarians expanded up into modern Ukraine, Russia, and Belarus, becoming the dominant population before the Viking expanded into the region starting around 800 AD. Somehow, the Slavs also picked up a large number of Sanskrit terms and concepts in the Conventional Indo-European Timeline, before they began to separate into different groups. This means that one must accept the idea that a group of Vedic Indians circa 1800 to 1100 BC CIET settled in Poland, and taught the Vedic religion to early Slavs and neighboring, but unrelated, Balts. They apparently had no contact either with the other Sanskrit-speaking peoples of India, but then did have contact with the Scythians living in Russia and Ukraine, as the later developments within Sanskrit did not affect the Slavic and Baltic languages, while the Scythian language did. Scythian was a language related to Avestan and more distantly, Persian, which left a clear imprint on the East Slavic languages, somehow, even though in the Conventional Indo-European Timeline the Scythians had been driven from Europe a thousand years before the Slavic languages began to separate.

On the other hand, in the Universal Long Timeline, all of the layers of cultural influence make perfect sense and correspond to archaeological evidence. The Proto-Balto-Slavic language would have developed in Belarus and neighboring regions within what archaeologists have labeled the Trzciniec-Komariv culture, between 1900 and 1200 BC. This language group would have been based on Mantra Sanskrit, which was previously spoken in the area by the Kurgan peoples, who themselves had begun migrating south to the Great Aral Sea. By the time that Balto-Slavic formed, the region was under the cultural domination of the Proto-Germanic Corded Ware culture, although the Germanic influence would have been limited so far to the east. The Balto-Slavic culture would have reached a peak, and likely started to separate into Baltic and Slavic groups under the Lusatian culture of Poland and Ukraine, circa 1300 to 500 BC. The following Pomeranian culture of the same region would have been the Proto-Slavic culture, between 650 and 150

BC. Around 300 BC a group of Slavs moved into the Scythian lands to the east as they headed south, where the remnants of their culture left the imprint on the Eastern Slavic dialect that formed in that region. This Eastern Slavic culture was the Przeworsk culture of the western Steppes, which lasted until around 500 AD, while the Slavs that stayed in the west formed the Oksywie-Wielbark culture between 200 BC and 400 AD. These two Eastern and Western Slavic cultures would have both been impacted by the environmental shift around 400 AD, and migrants would have flowed south into East Roman lands, where the South Slavic culture formed and the Old Slavonic alphabet was invented.

The Hattians and Hittites

ANATOLIAN ARCHAEOLOGICAL TIMELINE		
DYNASTIC PERIODS	**CMT**	**ULT**
Hattic Culture	Pre-2500 to 1664 BC	Pre-4000 to 3103 BC
Old Hittite Empire	1664 to 1524 BC	3103 to 2965 BC
Middle Hittite Kingdom	1524 to 1400 BC	2965 to 1450 BC
Mitanni Empire	1500 to 1300 BC	2967 to 1300 BC
New Hittite Empire	1400 to 1178 BC	
Middle Assyrian Kingdom	1178 to 912 BC	
Neo-Assyrian Empire	912 to 612 BC	

ANATOLIAN ARCHAEOLOGICAL TIMELINE	
REGIONAL SITES	CARBON-DATED TIMELINES
Natufian	13,050 to 7505 BC
Qaramel	13,000 to 6783 BC
Tell Abu Hureyra	13,000 to 5000 BC
Göbekli Tepe	9130 to 7370 BC
Nevalı Çori	8400 to 8100 BC
Çayönü	8630 to 6800 BC
Aşıklı Höyük	8200 to 7400 BC
Hassuna	7750 to 6780 BC
Çatalhöyük	7500 to 5700 BC
Tel Sabi Abyad	7500 to 5500 BC
Jarmo	7500 to 5000 BC
Bouqras	7400 to 6200 BC
Hacilar	7040 to 5000 BC

The Hattians are a little understood culture that existed in Anatolia before the Hittites moved into the region. Little of their culture survived the later expansion of the Hittites, who according to Akkadian records from the time slowly conquered the Hattians between approximately 3200 and 3103 BC ULT (1750 to 1664 BC CMT). As far as we can tell from the archaeological record, the Hattians were not a literate people, however, the Akkadians that were trading with them did record some of their names. These names have been interpreted by some as being Caucasian, distantly related to the modern Georgian and Abkhazian languages. This conclusion is far from accepted, however, there are no other competing theories, other than that the culture may not have survived to the present.

The Hattians are also often connected to the Hurrians that lived in northern Syria before the Mitanni and Assyrians conquering the area. This cultural affinity is generally accepted, however, the evidence is also limited as the Hurrian language was not recorded, other than in names recorded by the Akkadians, Hittites, Mitanni, Hyksos, and Assyrians. The Hattian culture was nevertheless highly advanced, being the first known culture in the region, or anywhere, that were engaging in iron-smelting, by as early as 4000 BC ULT (2500 BC CMT/CIET). This iron was used for jewelry, but not tools, which mirrors its use in many other ancient cultures. The predynastic and dynastic Egyptians used iron for jewelry since at least 5800 BC ULT (4000 BC CET), and in the Uruk period of Iraqi history since approximately the same time. Further north in the Samara culture on the Steppes of Eurasia, metal was only used as jewelry between 5500 and 3500 BC (as established by carbon dating).

The Hattian culture is also often connected to the ancient ruins in the region of southeast Turkey and northern Syria, and northern Iraq, such as Mureybet, Tell Abu Hureyra, Göbekli Tepe, Çayönü, Çatalhöyük, Hacilar, and Tell Sabi Abyad. Unfortunately, in the conventional timelines there is a significant gap between the ends of these civilizations, the last of which ended circa 5000 BC, and the earliest the Hattian culture can be firmly dated to, circa 2500 BC, or approximately 150 years before Sargon the Great of Akkad, circa 2334 BC CMT. This was not the foundation point of the Hattian civilization, but the earliest the civilization can be proven to be smelting iron, indicating that they were likely around for several centuries by 2500 BC, perhaps even a millennium, however, this is still a gap of 2500 years since the end of the last earlier civilizations. Using the Universal Long Timeline the Hattians began smelting iron circa 4000 BC ULT, which is a significantly shorter period of time than the 2500 year gap, but still not clear evidence that the cultures were connected.

These earliest archaeological sites do, however, support the Universal Long Timelines in proving that there were cities around when the Sumerians claimed there were, pre-dating the 1st Uruk Dynasty which began in Sumerian records circa 9868 BC. The Natufian Culture of the Levant, as well as the Tell Qaramel and Tell Abu Hureyra ruins, all date back to before 9868 BC, and other ruins in the region might as well, as very little archaeology has been done in the region due to ongoing ethnic violence and the rise and fall of the Islamic State.

The most famous site in the region is arguably Göbekli Tepe near the Syrian border of Turkey. The site was originally surveyed by a joint team from the Istanbul University and the University of Chicago in 1963, who, after doing virtually no work on the site, decided it was a Byzantine ruin from around a 1000 years ago, which is how it was listed until 1994 when Klaus Schmidt of the German Archaeological Institute decided to take a second look. He had been excavating nearby Nevalı Çori and was expecting to find other sites in the region that dated back to circa 8000 BC, and what he found when he excavated Göbekli Tepe quickly overturned the earlier assumption that it was a Byzantine gave yard. The upper layer which was first uncovered where scientifically dated to between 7560 and 7370 BC, and the earlier layers that have subsequently been uncovered have pushed the date back to 9130 to 8800 BC, however, these are just the three top levels. Some sites in the region have been shown to have dozens of distinct layers, and therefore very little is actually known about this culture. Additionally, ground-penetrating radar has shown that the site covers a large region around the hill that is the focus of the current work, and less than 5% of the site has been excavated. The other sites in the region have had even less work done on them, nevertheless, these archaeological sites prove there was civilization in Northern Mesopotamia by 10,000 BC, making the claims of the Sumerians at least plausible.

If there were civilizations spread across the Northern Mesopotamian region, it seems impossible that it did not trade along the Tigris and Euphrates, and therefore the question demands an answer: Where are the ruins of whoever the North Mesopotamians were trading with, if as Assyriologists insist, there was nothing in southern Iraq until circa 6500 BC. Are we to believe these people that did not have horses of the wheel, also did not know how to built boats, or even rafts? It is a scientific fact that people in the region have been using boats for at least 130,000 years, as that is when Crete was colonized,[37] yet, these advanced cultures 10,000 years ago had somehow forgotten that wood floats? Clearly, they were using the Tigris and Euphrates for trade as several sites are at the old courses of these rivers, and so, there must have been someone in southern Iraq at the time, as the Sumerian recorded.

---

[37]Strasser F. Thomas, et al. (2010) "Stone Age seafaring in the Mediterranean," *Hesperia (The Journal of the American School of Classical Studies at Athens)*, volume 79, pages 145-190

The Kassites, Mitanni and Hyksos

Regardless of when the Sumerian civilization started, it was eventually subsumed into the Akkadian culture. The first Akkadian king, Sargon the Great, conquered the Sumerians circa 3885 BC ULT (2334 BC CMT), and although there was brief Neo-Sumerian era circa 3568 to 3462 BC (2112 to 2004 BC), the Sumerian civilization died out, replaced by the various Semitic cultures that settled in Mesopotamia. These Semitic cultures built the Old Kingdoms of Babylonian and Assyrian empires between by 2965 BC ULT (1517 BC CMT). To the north the Hittites had conquered the Hattians and built their own empire by that time, however, then something happened, and these civilizations collapsed. The era that followed was a dark age in the Mesopotamian history of unknown length.

During this era when very little was recorded the Kassites conquered Babylon, and the Mitanni conquered the Assyrian Empire and most of the Hittite Empire. Both of these peoples are a general mystery, as they seem to have been illiterate when they invaded Mesopotamia and used the Babylonian and Assyrian languages for trade and diplomacy. The one known exception was when dealing with the Hittites, where they used the Hittite language. The Babylonians and Assyrians did leave some literature during this time, and it is clear from the names of these people, their gods, and the loan words that entered into the Semitic languages at the time, that these people were Indo-Aryans.

It has been argued that the gods of the Indo-Aryans were likely the same as the Avestan-speaking peoples, and therefore, these could have been any Indo-Iranian peoples, however, there are many names and terms, mainly to due with horses and chariots that are specifically Indo-Aryan, and not Iranian, and therefore most linguists have agreed that these were Indo-Aryans. This raises several problems for the conventional timelines, as the closes Sanskrit dialect appears to be Rigvedic or Mantra Language, which would mean that these Indo-Aryans would have to date to early in the period that the Vedic texts were being written in. This was explained by dating the Vedic texts to after 1800 BC CIET, however, with ironworking taking place in India by 2400 BC this dating is impossible, and therefore one has to assume a large group of Indo-Aryans somehow became cut-off from the rest for 1500 years as the Sanskrit language evolved, and then launched a massive invasion of Mesopotamia.

The fact that the Semitic peoples of Mesopotamia adopted Indo-Aryan terminology for horses and chariots is even more perplexing as they have already had the technology for almost a thousand years, as proven by the Standard of Ur, which showed horses and war-chariots in use in Sumer as early as 2600 BC, while in the convention timelines the Mitanni didn't conquer their empire until circa 1500 BC CMT, and Kassites didn't arrive in Babylon until 1570 BC CMT. One is left with the idea that for over 1000 years the Mesopotamians were using horses, wagons, and chariots but without ever naming them. The vision of these highly literate cultures simply pointing and grunting at horses and literally anything with a wheel for over a thousand years is apparently what Assyriologists want us to believe.

The situation is even more confusing when one adds the view of Egyptologists to the mix, as in the conventional Egyptian timeline has the Hyksos invading Egypt from North Mesopotamia circa 1674 BC, using horses and war-chariots, apparently, something the Egyptians had never encountered before, even though they were trading with the Sumerians since pre-dynastic times, and the Sumerians and later Mesopotamians had used horses and wagons for almost a thousand years by the time the Hyksos invaded. In fact, Egyptologists expect people to believe that the ancient Egyptians copied the concept of the ziggurat from the Egyptians, which is what the earliest pyramid: Djoser's Pyramid is, according to Egyptologists, yet, did not think to import horses, wagons, or even the wheel. For comparison, the Standard of Ur, which shows both the horse and the war-wagon is dated to circa 2600 BC by Assyriologists, while the entire Old Kingdom of Egypt, when all the largest pyramids were built, is dated to between 2685 and 2161 BC by Egyptologists. Compounding this bizarre timeline, the entire Middle Kingdom is dated to between 2061 and 1803 BC by Egyptologists, which is when the greatest work of environmental engineering ever done, was apparently done without and beasts of burden or even the wheel. This was the creation of the vast lake-land and terraced hills of the Fayum, in the desert east of Cairo. The Fayum is still part of the agricultural heartland of Egypt, however, at its height during the

Middle Kingdom the lake in the center, today called Lake Qarun, was 63 meters (about 207 feet) higher than it is today, and covered an area over ten times as large. This was accomplished by digging a canal to the Nile that allowed the annual floods to fill the area each year, all, without either using horses or wagons, both of which had been used by the Mesopotamians for 600 years.

This would be like Australia choosing to build a large sea in the interior of the outback, but choosing to do it using only technology that was widely available in the 1400s. One is left with the impression that the Egyptians must have been both the most brilliant engineers in all of history to do what they did, and the most idiotic engineers in all of history to do it the way they did it. Of course, this is only a valid perspective if the conventional Egyptian timeline is correct, which it clearly is not, as the Hyksos invading from Northern Mesopotamia circa 1674 BC, is impossible. The Hyksos were a Semitic people, with a Hurrian nobility, and some Indo-Aryan loanwords, and there was no culture like this in Mesopotamia, or anywhere else, until a couple of hundred years later. If the Hyksos traveled through Mesopotamia circa 1674 BC CMT, they did it at the height of the Old Babylonian, Old Assyrian, and Old Hittite Empires, and yet, no one noticed? Not only did no one in Mesopotamia notice them entering Egypt, but when the Egyptians finally drove them out in 1535 BC CET, no one in Mesopotamia noticed that either, even though the Old Assyrian and Old Hittite Empires were around at the time. In the conventional Mesopotamian timeline, the Babylonians had been conquered by the Kassites circa 1570 BC, however, they didn't notice this band of warriors passing through their territory either, and to put it in perspective, it is recorded that there were 480,000 Hyksos that were driven out of Egypt circa 1535 BC CET, not counting slaves. You'd think someone would notice an army of a half-million passing through their territory.

The simple truth is that the conventional timelines of Egypt and Sumer simply do not correlate. There was a culture in Mesopotamia exactly like the Hyksos, the latter Mitanni, but they didn't exist until late into the Mitanni era, when the local Hurrian culture had eclipsed the Indo-Aryan culture that conquered the empire, and that would have after 1500 BC CMT.

Naturally, none of these issues exist in the Universal Long Timeline, as the Kassites occupied Babylon circa 3013 BC ULT, introducing the horse, chariot, and terminology long before the Standard of Ur was created circa 2400 BC by one of the later Sea Dynasty kings. This is five hundred years after the chariot was apparently invented on the steppes by the earlier Kurgan/Indo-Aryans peoples. Some of these Indo-Aryans went on to conquer a large region of northern Mesopotamia over the next few decades, apparently, by freeing the Babylonian's Hurrian slaves, who then led insurrections in the Assyrian and Hittite Empires which the Indo-Aryans capitalized on, establish the Mitanni empire, or more properly confederation by 2967 BC ULT. Hundreds of years later, the Hyksos invaded Egypt in 2533 BC ULT, from the Mitanni confederation, and when they were ultimately driven from Egypt in 1731 BC ULT, they returned to the Mitanni confederation, which then fought a series of wars against their neighbors before being completely conquered in 1460 BC.

In the ULT, the Egyptians didn't choose to build the pyramids, dig the great canal, and terrace a region the size of Wales the hardest way imaginable because they, one would assume, had nothing better to do. They simply didn't have access to more advanced technology. In the ULT, the Kassites did not introduce wagon and chariot technology to the Mesopotamians until circa 3013 BC, while the Egyptian Middle Kingdom had collapsed circa 3249 BC.

The Harappans

Perhaps no archaeological ruins have been as hotly disputed as the Indus Valley Civilization, also called the Harappan Civilization after the initial ruin excavated: Harappa. The ruins of this civilization were discovered in the 1920s, and dated according to where they fit into the conventional Egyptian and Mesopotamian timelines, as there was no better method at the time. Subsequent attempts to carbon date the artifacts from the ruins have given such a wide and conflicting number of results that the data is essentially useless. It is clear that the Harappans were trading with the Sumerians from an early date, as Harappans artifacts have been found in Iraq dating to the 2nd Kish Dynasty, between 7025 and 4998 BC ULT (2700 to 2600 BC CMT). These artifacts were used to date the early Harappan Phase, Harappan 1, to circa 3300 to 2800 BC, and subsequently, the entire Indus Valley Civilization to between 3300 and 1300 BC, finishing up just before the beginning of the iron age circa 1200 BC, as there are no iron artifacts found in the ruins of this civilization. Of course, this is now an impossible range of dates for this civilization, as by 2400 there was ironworking in other parts of India, and by 1800 iron smelting in Uttar Pradesh state, which is within the region of this civilization, and by 1500 BC iron smelting had spread from India to Yaz in modern Turkmenistan, meaning it had to have traveled through the Indus civilization if it was still there. Yet, there is no iron found in this civilization's ruins, and therefore, it was not there at the time.

Using the Unified Long Timeline, the Harappan artifacts found in the 2nd King Dynasty from the Harappan 1 phase can be dated to roughly sometime between 7025 and 4998 BC ULT. Additional Harappan artifacts from the Harappan 3B phase have been found at Nippur corresponding to the life of Sargon the Great, which would be circa 3885 BC allowing for that phase to be roughly dated. The most recent Harappan artifacts found in Sumer date to the Isin Dynasty, circa 3462 to 3227 BC ULT, which are from the Harappan 3C phase. Harappan 3C was the last phase of the mature period of the Indus Civilization, which either went into sudden decline circa 1900 BC on the conventional Harappan timeline due to climatic changes that were entirely unique to Pakistan and India, or, went into sudden decline circa 3246 BC ULT as part of the global weather changes of 3250 BC, known as the Great Shock of 3250 BC. This was a period known from a number of sites and ice-cores from around the world, as a time period when the world's climate changed significantly into a neoglacial period that lasted until around 1500 BC. In the ULT it is linked with the collapse of the Egyptian Middle Kingdom, the Isin Dynasty in Iraq, the end of the Protopalatial period of Minoan civilization, and a number of migrations of various cultures in the Eurasian Steppes and Central Asia.

Indologists have estimated that there were approximately 600 years from the end of the Mature period until the ultimate demise of the Indus Civilization, which if applied to the ULT would place the end of this civilization circa 2846 BC, centuries before the time that ironworking appeared in southern

India. It also requires the Indus civilization to have existed by the 2nd King Dynasty, ending circa 4998 BC ULT, something that is inconsistent with Indologists' initial assumptions about when the culture formed. These early Indologist's assumptions were not simply based on correlations with the Sumerian and Akkadian civilizations, and the assumptions about the iron age starting in the Middle East somewhere, but also based on two centuries of research into the Vedas and more than a century of research into the *Avesta*. By the time that the ruins of the Indus Civilization were discovered both European and Indian scholars studying the ancient literature, had concluded that the origin of the Indo-Iranian peoples must be somewhere northwest of India, in Central Asia or Europe, and some went so far as to suggest the Indo-Iranians had originated in a sunken continent at the north pole. This idea, generally considered absurd today, was based on the fact that in the *Avesta* the 'High Watchpost' is built at a point around which the stars revolve. This was assumed to be the north pole, around which the stars at least appear to circle in the northern hemisphere. Additional texts were found that mentioned a day and a night lasting an entire year, which only happens in the polar regions, and resulted in the idea by 1900, that the Indo-Iranians had originated in the far north somewhere before migrating south into India.

This idea was by no means original, the Zoroastrians had migrated to India after Iran had become predominantly Islamic, and a thousand years before the Scythians had migrated to India from the Eurasian Steppes as the Goturks expanded into the region.

The idea that the Vedic Aryans had done the same at some point was a natural conclusion, however, some strongly disagree with this conclusion, claiming that all Indo-European peoples originate in India, not further north. This idea seems to have developed as an anti-Imperial view, even though there were Indian Nationalist that were involved with the scholarship that developed the theory that the Indo-Aryans migrated into India. At the time, in the late 1800s, there were no known ruins supporting this thesis, however, they were found throughout the 1900s, spread across the Eurasian Steppes.

In the view of the Out-of-India proponents, the ruins of the Indus Civilization are the ruins of the bronze age Vedic Civilization of the *Rig-veda*. This theory has yet to explain the lack of horses, chariots, yama graves, horse burials, and many other aspects of the *Rig-veda* that are lacking from the Indus ruins. The primary reason that so many Hindus believe that the Indus Valley Civilization is the ruins of the ancient Vedic Civilization, is due to the fact that the Indus Civilization is remarkably similar to the civilization described in the *Mahabharata*, *Ramayana*, and other great ancient Indian epics. The assumption among many Hindus is that this is the same civilization that wrote the Vedas, however, the Vedas and epics have virtually nothing in common.

The earliest Vedic texts have different heroes, gods, technology, and geography from the epics. Indologists theorize that the epics may have been translated from, or inspired by, older Dravidian language texts or stories dating from the Harappan civilization. Iravatham Mahadevan, the epigraphist who successfully deciphered the Tamil-Brahmi inscriptions, and who is world-renowned for his expertise on the epigraphy of the Indus Valley Civilization once described the situation as:

> "It is not a migrant civilization, it is not that a handful of settlers came and settled on the sea coast. This is a large, native, indigenous civilization. It is surprising that people hardly realize the extent of the Harappan civilization. It was more than a million square kilometers in area, much larger than modern Pakistan, much larger than all the other ancient civilizations, excepting China of course, put together. The Sumerian, the Akkadian, the Egyptian, Hittite and so on. Over such a large and fairly populous area, judging from the number of villages and cities. Several estimates of the population of Harappa and Mohenjo-daro have been made and they seem to have been very large cities by ancient standards. This only goes to confirm our supposition that you must look for a local language as a candidate for the Harappan script...

> ...the scale and the magnitude of the Harappan civilization speaks against its total extinction. As all scholars who have studied the problem agree, the incoming Aryans were relatively a very small minority and they were able to dominate only culturally and ultimately, in the assimilated Indo-Aryan or north Indian people, the indigenous racial element must have slowly surfaced. That is why we have no such thing as early Aryan pottery, because the pottery continued to be made by the local people. As someone has said jokingly, archaeology knows of no Aryans, only linguistics knows of Aryans. This is true. The

answer to this is that the incoming Aryans were small in number. In this respect there was no cultural discontinuity. The real discontinuity was in language, principally, and in religion and ritual in the earliest levels, but in later levels, modern Hinduism as we know it is a composite of both pre-Aryan, native, animistic and tribal religions and the incoming Aryan religion. Perhaps when the Indus script is deciphered, I would not be surprised to find that the greater part of modern Hinduism has a Harappan lineage."[38]

Traditional Hindu gods found in the epics began to appear in the Vedas in the Brahmana Prose sections, which in the ULT would have been written in Iron Age India between 1800 and 1100 BC, meaning they would have been living among the Dravidian speaking ancient Hindus of the Harappan civilization by this point. For example, the Shatapatha Brahmana in the *Yajur-veda* contains the earliest mention of Garuda in the Vedas, in the Brahmana Prose. The *Mahabharata*, which is believed to have been written between the 7th century BC and 4th century AD, claims that Garuda is also Garutman, who was in the Rigveda, and therefore Hindus generally accept that Garuda was in the Rigveda. Likewise, other epic gods, heroes, and geographic locations have been spliced into the early Vedic Texts by simply stating that the names in the Vedic Texts are another set of names for the same gods, heroes, and geographic locations found in the epics. This is naturally, an undisprovable hypothesis if any name simply means whatever you want it to, then any text could have

---

[38]Iravatham Mahadevan (1998) "Ancient Indus Valley Script" Interview by Omar Khan

been written anytime, and be about anyone. By this logic, the Torah could have been written by ... Confucius? Why not?

The fact is, the ancient Indian epics are clearly based in India, but the Vedas were not. The Vedas were written by people who used the horse, while the epics were written by people who lived along rivers, and traveled by boat. Horses and iron, and even airplanes have been added to the epics, but there is no reason to believe they were not added at a later date, as the oldest known versions are believed to have been first written in Classical Sanskrit, long after the Indo-Aryans would have settled in northern India, and brought their horses with them. The airplanes are a curious addition to the epics, but not a recent addition, although the translation of the word 'vimana' as 'airplane' was developed after the invention of the airplane in the early-1900s. Older English to Sanskrit dictionaries translated 'vimana' as 'flying car,' 'flying carriage,' or 'flying machine,' and some scholars postulated that these were references to a carriage mounted on the backs of elephants, although there is no evidence of this in the texts themselves. As some vimanas were said to travel to other planets, or be the size of cities, the elephant-carriage hypothesis is generally considered as a plausible inspiration for the idea, but in most surviving texts, historians generally view vimanas as purely literary devices intended to show the power of the gods.

Horses and chariots far more common in the epics than elephants, however, the technology found in the epics, other than the flying machines, reflects the technology of Iron Age India, when they were likely first written, at least in the Sanskrit language. These epics are generally considered by Hindus to be accurate descriptions of ancient events, and Indologists generally are willing to accept the idea that the stories are set in the ancient Indus Valley Civilization, even if the stories are themselves later fiction. In most respects, the culture and geography described in the ancient epics match what Indologists think the Indus Civilization was like. Major characters are often described as having dark skin, which Dravidian people have, and many names are believed to be Dravidian loan-words.

Hanuman, the monkey-god: The orientalist F. E. Pargiter theorized that Hanuman the monkey-demigod from the epics was a proto-Dravidian deity, and the name 'Hanuman' was a Sanskritization of the Old Tamil words *Aan-mandhi* meaning 'male monkey.' The Hindu scholar Ray Govindchandra influenced by Pargiter's opinion suggested in 1976 that the early Indo-Aryans may have invented a Sanskrit etymology for the deity's name after they accepted Hanuman in their pantheon.[39] Garuda, the name of the eagle-god does not appear to be a Sanskrit word and is not found in the Vedas until the Shatapatha Brahmana in the Yajurveda, written in Brahmana Prose after the Indo-Aryans would have migrated into India. In the earlier sections of the Vedas, a similar creature called Śyena is found, which is the Sanskrit word for eagle. The name Garuda is believed to be based on the old Dravidian word *karug-u* mean-

---

[39]Philip Lutgendorf (2007) *Hanuman's Tale: The Messages of a Divine Monkey.* Page 40

ing 'eagle,'[40] and therefore many Hindus view this as the same character. Even if it is, the shift in the name shows that the Indo-Aryans had come under a strong enough Dravidian influence that they were changing the names of their own gods to fit into the new culture they were surrounded by.

The changing of one's god's name is no small affair, but does happen. Most Christians living in the Middle East call their god Allah, which in Arabic translates as 'the God.' While this is a perfectly valid translation of any monotheistic god, it is an Islamic title, and therefore something the Middle Eastern Christians adopted from the Muslims, and something not noted in the Middle East until almost a thousand years after the time of Mohamed. A similar transition has taken place in Southeast Asia, were in nations that have become mainly Islamic, older Hindu literature has been Islamized, for example, Allah has replaced Brahma in local versions of the *Ramayana*.[41] This transition only took a few hundred years, however, it also included the adoption of a new religion, which the Vedic people do not appear to have done.

Unlike the Vedas, there is no surviving literary evidence for the epics before Classical Sanskrit, although there is a general acceptance that at least the core of the story must be much older. This is a strong indicator that the epics were translated at

---

[40]Robert Caldwell (1996) *A Comparative Grammar of the Dravidian Or South-Indian Family of Languages*, Third Edition, Page 591

[41]Gauri Mahulikar (2001) *Effect of Ramayana on various cultures and civilisations*

that point into Sanskrit, which is why Old Dravidian names and places in the Indus Civilization are described. The setting of the *Mahabharata* is northern India and Pakistan, approximately 3200 to 3100 BC. This fact has never been in doubt, even before archaeologists actually found ruins in the region that date to that time. Before that, it was simply considered, by non-Hindus, a fictional tale designed to present the central thesis of the Bhagavad Gita, which is the philosophical view of Krishna that takes up a quarter of the text. Since the discovery of ruins in the region the *Mahabharata* was set in and dating to the time period, the fictional assumption is now questioned by many, although like many early assumptions by Indologists, Assyriologists, and Egyptologists, it is still generally accepted as some sort of divine inspiration by the followers of those cult-like disciplines.

In the *Mahabharata*, Krishna and his brothers the Yadavas were driven from their home town of Mathura when the city was attacked, and occupy the ancient island fortress formerly called Kushasthali, which they rebuilt[42] and renamed Dwarka.[43] This fortress served as their base and home through the ensuing war, and after their ally, King Arjuna had won, there were a few decades of peace. However, a fight broke out between the Yadava brothers, which resulted in them all dead, and when Arjuna hear this, he ordered Dwarka to be abandoned, following which it sank into the sea. The island didn't simply

---

[42]Kisari Mohan Ganguli, translator (1893) *Mahabharata* 2.14.50
[43]Vettam Mani (2010) *Puranic Encyclopaedia*, 9th Reprint, Page 89

become abandoned and eventually sink into the sea, the event leading up to it was described quite traumatically:

> *"Winds, dry and strong, and showing gravels, blew from every side. Birds began to wheel, making circles from right to left. The great rivers ran in opposite directions. The horizon on every side seemed to be always covered with fog. Meteors, showering (blazing) coals, fell on the Earth from the sky. The Sun's disc, O king, seemed to be always covered with dust. At its rise, the great luminary of day was shorn of splendour and seemed to be crossed by headless trunks (of human beings). Fierce circles of light were seen every day around both the Sun and the Moon. These circles showed three hues. These edges seemed to be black and rough ans ashy-red in colour. These and many other omens, foreshadowing fear and danger, were seen, O king, and filled the hearts of men with anxiety."*[44]

The traditional dating of Krishna's life is between 3228 and 3102 BC. Completely coincidentally, 3,103 BC is the year the Hittite Empire was founded in the ULT, and given that the Hittites conquered the much older and more technologically advanced Hattians, something significant must have happened to cause them to suddenly become aggressive. As the Middle Egyptian Kingdom had collapsed by 3100 BC ULT, we only have fragmented record from the time, however, there is one text that is sometimes dated to the 13th dynasty, the inscriptions in the tomb of Ankhtifi in Mo'alla. This text is generally dated to

---

[44]Kisari Mohan Ganguli, translator (1893) *Mahabharata*, Book 16

the end of the 8th Dynasty and may date to that period, however, there is no evidence to support it either way, and internal evidence can also be used to date it to the 13th Dynasty.

> *"...I fed Hefat (the town of Mo'alla), Hormer, and [gap in text] in the time when the sky was storms and the land was in the sandstorms of starvation on this sandbank of the Hell (tzw – the Underworld where Apophis, the great serpent, that tried to eat the Sun)."*

Little is known from Ankhtifi's life, other than that when he was young, Abydos was still the residence of the Overseer of Upper Egypt, and by the end of his life there was no longer an Overseer of Upper Egypt, and Ankhtifi was the nomarch (count) of Hierakonpolis and Edfu, two of Egypt's southernmost nomes (counties). Whenever Ankhtifi lived, it appears to be at the collapse of a kingdom, which would either mean either the 7th/8th dynasty or 13th dynasty, however, Abydos was not abandoned in the 7th/8th dynasty, yet was abandoned during the 13th dynasty, so why do Egyptologists date it to the 8th dynasty. Simply put, Egyptologists have compressed the 1666 years of the Second Egyptian Dark Age (Second Intermediate Period) into 254 years, forcing multiple dynasties to coexist, creating a complicated mess of competing dynasties that even sometimes used the same capital city at the same time. As a result, there just isn't any time for Ankhtifi's life, and the storms and sandstorms and famine that led to the collapse of Abydos, so Ankhtifi's life is moved to the First Egyptian Dark Age, even though Abydos survived that dark age.

If in fact, Ankhtifi's life was at the beginning of the 13th Dynasty, then he would have lived between approximately 3246 and 3200 BC ULT, at the same time as the traditional dating of Krishna's life. The specific date of the birth of Krishna was calculated by the Indian mathematician and astronomer Aryabhatta in the early 6th century AD, based on the astronomical references found in the *Mahabharata*, and while the date of his death is also attributed to Aryabhatta it is unclear where it came from, as the *Mahabharata* only mentioned the alignment of the planets when Krishna was born, not when he died. As Krishna lived so long ago, and the earliest written copy of his life was written in Classical Sanskrit, one must allow for errors in transmission. It was translated, at least once before being written in Sanskrit, and no doubt copied hundreds of times before that in the original language if it was written before that. If it wasn't written before that, then it must have been recited, meaning hundreds of people would have had to learn the story and repeat it verbatim for thousands of years.

Likewise, the records of the ancient Egyptians cannot be accepted as exactly correct down to the year or even decade either due to the gaps that exist in the dark ages, and therefore, these two events could be the same event. If so, then the time of Krishna would be circa 3246 BC in the Universal Long Timeline.

Above and below are two pictures of the ruins in Harappa, the above photograph showing a close-up of the foreground area of the below photograph.

According to all ancient sources, the author of the *Mahabharata* was the scribe Vyasa Dwaipayana, who lived sometime between 5000 and 4000 years ago, and was said to have been born on an island in the Yamuna River, which is a major tributary of the Ganges in northern India. This places him in the Harappan 1 Phase of the Indus Valley Civilization according to the Conventional Harappan Timeline, and the Harappan 5 Phase in the ULT, so either way Vyasa lived in the Indus Valley Civilization, which included the western Ganges region where the Yamuna River is located, assuming he is not fictional, as most Indologists seem willing to accept.

Above is a photo of the 'Pre-Harappan' ruins of Mehrgarh.

The island of Dwarka where Krishna and his brothers lived was located off the coast of western India, near the modern city of Dwarka, and does exist as a sunken island with a stone fortress on it, and it is not the only ruin located off the coast of northwest India. In the Gulf of Khambhat, another ruin was discovered in 2001, which has been studied in more detail. This ruin is the remains of a stone metropolis 9 kilometers long, which ran along an ancient shoreline that is now around 40 meters below the waterline, and debris found within it has been carbon-dated to between 7545 and 7490 BC.[45] It

---

[45]S. Kathiroli (2004) "Recent Marine Archaeological Finds in Khambhat, Gujarat," *Journal of Indian Ocean Archaeology*, 2004 Pages 141-149

seems improbable that this metropolis is unrelated to the ruins of the Indus Valley Civilization or the earlier Mehrgarh Civilization, however, in the Conventional Harappan Timeline there is a gap of 4200 years between this metropolis and the Indus Valley Civilization, and 500 years before the Mehrgarh Civilization's early phase.

Above are two photos of the ruins in the Gulf of Khambhat, which show their similarity to the ruins of Harappa, Mehrgarh, and Bhirrana.

Conversely, in the Unified Long Timeline, this coastal metropolis still existed during about 2700 years before the Harappan 1 Phase, however, at the same time as Mehrgarh Civilization's early phase. Several specific artifacts can be used to correlate the Harappan civilization with the Unified Long Timeline, including the Harappan artifacts recovered from Susa, Nippur, and Kish in Sumeria, and the assumed time-period life of Krishna. Only one artifact can be dated to a specific historical person, an artifact from the Harappan 3C phase found in Nippur believed to date to the time of Sargon the Great, king of Akkad, who seized control of Mesopotamia circa 3885 BC ULT. An artifact from the Harappan 3C phase was found in Susa, which would have to date to before the end of the Isin dynasty circa 3227 BC ULT. The earliest Harappan artifact found in Iraq was found in the ruins of Kish, which in the ULT existed from 7025 BC onward, and therefore this artifact could date to anytime before Sargon the Great.

Using the general outline of the Indus Valley Civilization that has been worked out by Indologists, and assuming the life of Krishna was circa 3246 BC ULT, correlating with both the collapse of the Egyptian Middle Kingdom and the end of the Harappan Mature Phase, then the general framework places the Indus Valley Civilization as between 6546 and 2846 BC ULT. Using this timeline, the artifacts found in Mesopotamia do correlate with the Harappan phases they are believed to date to. There can be little doubt that future excavations in India will support the Universal Long Timeline, and hopefully find enough of the Indus Valley Script that we can confirm the stories found in the Classic Sanskrit epics do date to those civilizations.

An additional factor worth considering from a historical perspective, but considered sacrilegious by many Hindus, is the date of life of Rama. Rama was the hero of the *Ramayana*, which exists in over a dozen significant variations across South and Southeast Asia. While the story, which includes everything from mermaids to space stations in some version, might be largely fictional, it is clearly an ancient story. The hero-king Rama is generally believed to be the king of India that the ancient Greeks and

Romans reported as King Dionysus. As early as 1784, Sir William Jones pointed out the clear correlations between the Indian King the Greeks called Dionysus and Rama, consider the following two quotes from his essay '*On the Gods of Greece, Italy, and India.*'

> "*Meros is said by the Greeks to have been a mountain of India, on which their Dionysus was born, and that Meru is also a mountain near the city of Naishada, or Nysa, called by the Grecian geographers Dionysopolis, and universally celebrated in the Sanskrit poems.*"

> "*...deems Rama to be the same as the Grecian Dionysos, who is said to have conquered India with an army of satyrs, commanded by Pan; and Rama was also a mighty conqueror, and had an army of large monkeys or satyrs, commanded by Maruty, son of Pavan. Rama is also found, in other points, to resemble the Indian Bacchus.*"

The 'Maruty, son of Pavan' was Hanuman, using an older translation of the name. The idea that Rama was considered important in the time of the Greco-Roman civilization is not in doubt, as the *Ramayana* dates back to at least this time, however, what is relevant is what the Greek and Roman historians recorded about the date of his life. All Greco-Roman records of Rama, or the Indian Dionysus, or the India Bacchus, depending on the language of the author, place Rama's life at approximately 6,451 years before the time of Alexander the Great, and that there were 154 kings that ruled between them. This would be approximately 6600 BC, before the Indus Valley Civilization existed, yet during the Mehrgarh Civilization. This is not what Hindus generally believe, as the current Hindu calculation for his life places it over 2 million years ago. While the Greco-Roman historians like Pliny[46] and Arrian[47] were clearly quoting an Indian source that had access to a significant King list, that source no longer exists. Naturally, just because people believed something 2000 years ago, does not mean it is accurate, however, the fact that there are ruins from the region, dating to the time of these 154 kings does at least make their existence plausible, as someone built those cities.

On the following page is a photograph of the 'Pre-Harappan' ruins of Bhirrana.

---

[46]Pliny the Elder (79 AD) *Naturalis Historia*, 6.59-60
[47]Arrian of Nicomedia (circa 150 AD) *Indica*, 9.9

Brahmi and Kharosthi

Many Vedic gods found their way into the Classic Sanskrit epics, but generally as vague heavenly beings that were only peripherally involved in the stories being told, such as the Vedic Aruna, the personification of the sun-rise from the Vedic Texts, that incarnated as Aruni, a woman who gave birth to two monkey-men in the epics. Not only is are these two unrelated stories, but if there wasn't a similarity of the name no one would ever connect them. Comparing the red-glow of sun-rise to a woman who gives birth to monkey-men, is like comparing the Moon to a ... woman who gives birth to monkey-men.

While the Vedic gods were added to the much later epics does not seem difficult to understand, the fact that they were added so 'inconsistently' as Indologists call it, draws into question just how many people were still even aware of who they were by the Classical Sanskrit era, as most seem to simply be the reuse of the older names, completely unconnected to what the Vedic god actually was. On the other hand, the appearance of the epic gods and heroes in the Vedas allows confirmation that the latter sections of the Vedas were written within the Dravidian speaking culture then dominant in northern India.

The name Rama appears in the *Atharva-veda*, however, it wasn't a name but a descriptive term, meaning dark-colored or black.[48] There is a mention of 'Devaki's son Krishna' in the Chandogya Upan-

---

[48]Monier Monier Williams (1899) *Sanskrit English Dictionary with Etymology*, Page 877, राम

ishad of the *Sama-veda*, however, this is written in Sutra Language, which would place its origin in India between 1100 and 600 BC. It is generally assumed that this was a reference to the Krishna from the *Mahabharata*, although the reference is vague. Both Garuda and Vishnu are mentioned in the *Rig-veda*, but again in the Brahmana Prose sections, like Garuda, which date to between 1800 and 1100 BC ULT. Vishnu, today one of Hinduism's supreme deities, was not a major god in either the epics or the *Vedas*, however, based on when he entered into the *Rig-veda*, must have been a Harappan god, although, he appears to be somewhat like the Vedic gods in the epics, and may represent another ancient tradition within South Asia that was also being grandfathered into the epics. Brahma was not mentioned in the Vedic texts until the Maitrayaniya Upanishad of the *Yajur-veda*, which was composed in Sutra Language, and would, therefore, date to between 1100 and 600 BC ULT. The word shiva exists in the Vedas, but as an epithet meaning 'auspicious,' often linked with the Vedic gods Rudra, or Indra, or Angi. As a result, some Hindus believe that Shiva is Rudra, while others believe he was Indra, and others believe he was Angi. As it is logical to assume the Vedic texts did shape the evolution of Hinduism after they became part of Hinduism, the modern Shiva likely drew from all of them, however, a god named Shiva was not mentioned in the Vedic Texts.

Clearly, a great deal of what is today Hinduism is drawn from the Vedic Texts, such as the Rigvedic concept of Atman, however, the earliest Vedic Texts were not created in the same region or culture as the ancient Sanskrit epics. The epics as they exist today, are generally dated by scholars and linguists to the Classic phase of the Sanskrit language before various regional languages rose in India to supplant Sanskrit. Classical Sanskrit was based on the Aṣṭādhyāyī treatise of the ancient Indian grammarian Pāṇini. It is unclear exactly when Pāṇini lived, however, his life is generally dated to between the 7th and 4th-century BC. The various dating methods used for his life are tragically pointless, for example, at one point he mentioned writing in the Aṣṭādhyāyī, which has led many scholars to assume he lived after the Greek conquered Pakistan and introduced the Greek alphabet, meaning he would have to have been alive as late as approximately 320 BC. This is a preposterously-ignorant argument for an academic to make, as the Greeks simply conquered the Persian Empire, which was literate, and had previously annexed parts of Pakistan by 540 BC. Moreover, the ancient Indus Valley Civilization had a form of writing which Indologists acknowledge was in use since at least 3000 BC, yet, the Greeks introduced writing to India after 320 BC?

Little is truly known about the life and death of Pāṇini. It is believed he was born in northern Pakistan to a woman named Dākṣī, and was killed by a lion, much later, in between he reinvented the Sanskrit language. Pāṇini's Aṣṭādhyāyī was the most advanced grammatical standard ever produced in the ancient world, and made use of a technical metalanguage consisting of a syntax, morphology, and lexicon. There was nothing like it ever produced for the Persian, Greek, or Latin languages. Grammarians did not come close to reproducing work like it until the 1700s, and even then it is arguable. As it sits, the dating of Pāṇini's life is largely based around the question of when Classical Sanskrit emerged and Sutra Language Sanskrit stopped being used. It was believed universally in ancient times that he lived before Siddhartha Gautama, the Buddha. However, with the entire evolution of the Sanskrit language forced to date to after the Mediterranean Iron Age, circa 1200 BC, this became impossible, and each new generation finds a way to shift him a century or so forward in time, in a few decades he'll probably be that guy that Gandhi knew, after all, if he wasn't talking about Indian writing, or Persian writing, why assume he was talking about Greek writing? English, obviously he was talking about English! Hey, Gandhi knew English... Seriously, the methods used to date his life are that haphazard.

The other piece of internal evidence that was originally used to date Pāṇini's life to after Siddhartha's, before linguists caught on the to maybe 'writing' meant 'Greek' idea, was that in the *Aṣṭādhyāyī* Pāṇini mentioned 'kumāraśramaṇa' which as the Buddhist version of nuns, so clearly this was after the life of Siddhartha. But Siddhartha did not invent nuns, or even Buddhism! Siddhartha was a buddha, which means 'teacher,' but not the first buddha in any school of Buddhism, in fact, some schools claim the first Buddha lived over 50,000 years ago! Additionally, the Jain religion, which existed long before Siddharta's life also has nuns, called kumāraśramaṇa, meaning this argument that Buddha invented nuns was as feeble-minded as the

Greek idea. However, none of these preposterous ideas would have even been proposed if scholars weren't forced to date all of Sanskrit's evolution, which linguistically should have taken thousands of years, to just a few hundred.

The issue of 'writing' is even more complicated by the question of not just which script was he talking about, but, did he know how to write himself? Which is a bit like asking did Einstein actually know how to do mathematics, or did he just see some people doing it, and say "Huh, math? Anyway, did you know E=MC2?" Pāṇini's *Aṣṭādhyāyī* is undeniably the greatest known grammatical treatise of the ancient world, and yet it is debated whether he bothered to write it down, or just mentioned his musing to some people he knew. Seriously? Yes! It is hotly debated, because, you know... Greek anyone?

The core issue is the fact that virtually no writing exists from ancient India. This does not mean that ancient Indians were not writing, just that if they were, the texts have not survived to the present. There are clay tablets and some engraved stones in the ruins of the Indus Valley Civilization, and there are some later engravings on rocks, but there are no surviving paper, papyrus, parchment, vellum, or palm-leaf texts surviving to the time of Pāṇini. In South Asia, the most common writing medium has been palm-leaves, but due to the humidity across the subcontinent the leaves generally deteriorate within a decade, and therefore someone needs to be constantly making copies in order for the texts to not be lost. Any interruption of the copiest's work would lead to the rapid disappearance of the text. So, wars, storms, and everything in between have ravaged almost all ancient Indian literature, and even major works like the Vedas and epics have regional differences as portions have been lost in some areas.

The question of which script Pāṇini was talking about, is central to the question of when Pāṇini lived, and if one is forced to accept that all of Sanskrit's dialects evolved and supplanted the former dialects within a few centuries, which the conventional Indo-European timeline demands, mainly due to the Mitanni presence in Mesopotamia circa 1500 BC CMT, then one needs Classical Sanskrit to be as recent as possible in order to leave as much time as possible for the old Sanskrit dialects to have formed and been abandoned. However, the conventional timelines contain far too many inconsistencies to be taken seriously and in the ULT there is more than enough time for Pāṇini to have lived before Siddhartha.

The life of Siddhārtha Gautama is universally date to sometime between 563 and 400 BC, although the specific years are debated. This means that Classical Sanskrit was in use for approximately 1000 years when it was finally replaced by the emergence of regional dialects. This timeline of Sanskrit in India parallels the thousand years of Latin in Western Europe before it was replaced by regional dialects, and the thousand years of Classical Arabic before it was replaced by regional dialects. There is no thousand-year rule about the regionalization of languages, however, the parallels are notable. Clearly, in Europe, the regionalization of the Romance languages was influenced by the collapse of the Roman Empire, and invasions of Germanic tribes, as the collapse of the Caliphate and the invasions of Mongols and Turks no doubt impacted the regionalization of Arabic. In India, the cause of the regionalization is less clear, however, is generally tied to the collapse of the Gupta Dynasty, and the invasions of the Huns from Central Asia.

However, unlike what happened in Europe with the fracturing of Latin into the Romance languages, which nevertheless continued to use the Latin alphabet, in India, the Sanskrit-derived Indo-Aryan language each developed a unique script. This points to the Indians being in at least one way, very different from the Europeans of the time, as the Indians obviously had a relatively high literacy rate. In Western Europe, as Christianity took over, literacy rates fell. This was caused by a number of specific causes, such as mass deaths from diseases that were rampant at the time, but also as Christians actively burned libraries, something the Indians apparently did not do, at least on the same scale. The maintenance of the Latin alphabet was due to the fact that there was very little literacy in any West European language, and so West Europeans that wanted to read and write did so in Latin. In India, the rapid regionalization of the Brahmi script into local scripts was possible due to the fact that texts needed to be rewritten constantly, and so each new development of the script would be standard across all texts in that language within a decade or so.

The script being used in India the Classical era of Greco-Roman civilization was the Brahmi script, which looks vaguely like Greek, which is where the idea that the Indians learned to write from the Greeks came from, however, the ancient Greeks themselves never reported this, it is a theory proposed in the 1700s. The majority of Brahmi script carvings that have been found are from Northern India and are written in Sanskrit, however, this is not the only Indian language written in Brahmi, there are also Brahmi carvings in Tamil and Ceylonese in Southern India and Sri Lanka, which date back to the same period. Since the 1970s the idea that the Brahmi script even originated in Northern India has come under attack by Tamils and Sri Lankans, although that had always been the assumption. The oldest Sanskrit Brahmi carvings that can be firmly dated in Northern India date to around 250 BC, while in Southern India Tamil Brahmi inscriptions have been both radiometrically and carbon-dated to dated between 520 and 490 BC, and in Sri Lanka the Ceylonese Brahmi inscriptions are dated to around the same time.

Naturally, this does not prove that the script was invented in Southern India and adopted by the northerners, however, that is one possibility. The more relevant fact is that three versions of Brahmi were already different at the earliest point we have found examples of them. Both the Tamil and Ceylonese variants had symbols for sounds made in Dravidian languages that are not present in Indo-Aryan languages, although the language written in the Ceylonese Brahmi script was Indo-Aryan, it obviously had a large number of Dravidian loanwords. Wherever this script originated, it had already been adopted and adapted by two, possibly three, cultures circa 500 BC, and therefore must have been in use in at least one of these cultures for a significant period of time. Somewhere, a culture had developed this script, and become so influential that their neighbors or trading partners started using the script, and by 500 BC it may have already been spread across the Indian subcontinent and was clearly widespread in the south.

	-a	-ā	-i	-ī	-u	-ū	-e	-o
k-								
kh-								
g-								
gh-								
ṅ-								
c-								
ch-								
j-								
jh-								
ñ-								
ṭ-								
ṭh-								
ḍ-								
ḍh-								
ṇ-								
t-								
th-								
d-								
dh-								
n-								
p-								
ph-								
b-								
bh-								
m-								
y-								
r-								
l-								
v-								
ś-								
ṣ-								
s-								
h-								
ḷ-								

The Brahmi script was a fairly complex script in comparison to the Phoenician, Aramaic, Greek, and Latin scripts used to the west, and bore no resemblance to the older Egyptian, Cuneiform, or Chinese scripts. Brahmi is an abugida in which each letter represents a consonant, while vowels are written with an obligatory diacritic. The following is a chart of the symbols used in around 250 BC when the Greeks first translated it. Each of the 34 consonants could have one of 8 diacritics which means there were a total of 272 symbols. This is a notable difference from the 24 letters of the Greek alphabet, 21 letters of the archaic Latin alphabet, 22 letters of the Phoenician abjad, and 22 letters of the Aramaic abjad.

The difference between Brahmi and the western scripts is so significant it is difficult to believe that anyone could think Brahmi is based on the western alphabets, regardless of whether there are some physical similarities in the shapes of some Brahmi symbols and Greek letters. In the end, there are only so many shapes that one can quickly draw, and most alphabets have some similar symbols in them. As complex as the 272 symbols may seem, the system is remarkably simple once learned, and provides exacting and very specific sounds, unlike Latin, which requires accents and additional symbols to represent most languages, or, clairvoyance in the case of English, which is impossible to sound out without first learning the language. Which sound does the letter J correspond to in English, or G, C, S, V, W, D, T, Y, X, A, O, E, I, Y, U, or R? It depends on the local dialect, and the actual sounds may be reversed in one country versus another, such as V and W in Indian versus American English, the completely different pronunciation of R in British versus Canadian English. In Brahmi this was not possible, however, that is also why so many scripts developed from it as the languages fragmented.

The various Mediterranean scripts that were used in the iron age are all believed to be derived from the Phoenician script, as the Phoenicians colonized the Mediterranean during the iron age, and traded with everyone. The Greek, Latin, Aramaic, Tifinagh, Etruscan, and other Mediterranean scripts are all believed to be based on Phoenician and generally work the same way, either as an abjad or an alphabet, and either way with only 22 to 26 letters, nothing complex like Brahmi. The origin of the Phoenician script is itself unknown, however, it has variously been traced to ancient Egyptian Hieroglyphs or Hieratic, Minoan Linear-A, or the Proto-Sinaitic script, which itself is virtually unknown. The wide-scale adoption and adaption of the Phoenician script throughout the Mediterranean, even replacing older scripts like Linear-B and Cuneiform is believed to have happened because it was simple, which contradicts the idea that Brahmi developed from it, or its child scripts Aramaic and Greek.

Like the western scripts, Brahmi is a system of abstract symbols, however, there is no surviving pictographic phase. In all known regions where writing was developed, it was preceded by a pictographic system. In Egyptian, Hierarchic developed from Hieroglyphs, and then later developed into the more abstract Demotic. In Iraq, Cuneiform developed from

107

a pictographic script which was itself preceded by small clay tokens in the image of birds, fish, and cow's heads. Chinese Characters developed from an earlier system of pictograms which have been found on ancient Chinese oracle bones. Minoan Hieroglyphs were in use before the development of the Linear-A script. There is debate about where the shift first took place, and which ancient script influenced which, but the pattern of development was identical, and even if the Sumerian, Egyptian, and Minoan systems of writing were all influencing each other, Chinese is believed to have developed in isolation, much like Mayan in the Americas.

A similar development process can be seen in the Mayan script, which developed from pictures into a collection of glyphs, which while still resembling pictures and sometimes used to mean the picture depicted, also meant specific sounds in the Mayan language, allowing for the pronunciation of abstract concepts which cannot be drawn. This jump from drawing a fish or a cow-head, to having sounds that represent abstract concepts is what separates a series of pictures from a written script. Many concepts cannot be drawn, like blue, or cold, or 'this is how you bake bread.' Pictures and tokens can still be useful, if a token of a cows head can be exchanged for a cow, then it is essentially money but does not allow the expression of stories that can be read thousands of years later. Human remains date back hundreds of thousands of years, but if our ancestors were telling epic tales back then, those stories are lost forever, yet, some of what the Sumerians and Egyptians recorded still survives, due to the leap from pictures to symbols.

On the other hand, Brahmi simply appears, fully formed in its earliest known varieties, indicating that the majority of its developmental history must be missing. It is clear that it was not being carved into the sides of massive stone blocks like in Egypt, or pressed and baked into clay tablets like in Mesopotamia, and therefore one is left with the notion that the script was mainly used for writing on palm leaves, or some other medium that has been lost to time. Of course if one assumes that someone was writing something, one is still left with the question of what? Brahmi was not a simple writing system designed for scratch names and lists of items like the Phoenician script. Brahmi was clearly designed artificially or developed over a long period, to exactly replicate the entire range of sounds that were possible, with 272 just for the Sanskrit language. This means that the entire range of human thoughts and ideas could have been written in the language. In Phoenician and other abjads there are a large number of sounds that are implied, which is fine if you know the language, but leads to many debates among linguists today as we cannot be sure what many of the words mean.

Abjads do not include letters for the vowels, and therefore even well known ancient texts written in abjads can be confusing. For example, the Jewish Torah, which is one of the most well studied ancient texts, yet the meaning of approximately a quarter of the words is unclear. There are accepted assumptions about what they mean, and a great deal of debate within Rabbinical literature going back over a thousand years. Christian translators usually fall back to the ancient Greek translation done at the Library of Alexandria when they aren't she what a word means, however even the ancient Greeks didn't always know what the words meant. A simple example of this is found near the beginning of the Torah, in Genesis 1:21: גדול תנין. What do these two words mean? The ancient Greeks translated them as 'great whales,' as they did not know what the Torah said. This translation was subsequently placed into the King James translation, as the language professors at Oxford did not know what the words meant. Depending on the translation גדול can mean *great, large, number, intense, loud, older, important, god, or haughty*, while תנין can mean *dragon, dinosaur, sea monster, river monster, serpent*, or *snake*, but not a *whale*. So what do these two words mean: *the great dragon, large dinosaur, number of sea monsters, intense river monster, loud serpent, older snake, important dragon, dinosaur god, haughty sea monster*, or some other thing entirely? None of this vagary was possible using the Brahmi script.

To farther complicate the issue for scripts in Northern India, there was another script used to write Sanskrit, and it was at least partly based on Aramaic. This other Sanskrit script is called Kharosthi and was in use in Pakistan alongside Brahmi when the Greeks conquered the region, and continued in use until the 3rd century AD, dying out a couple of centuries before Brahmi in South Asia, however, continued in use in Central Asia until the 7th-century. Like Brahmi, Kharosthi was an abugida, however, it was influenced by Aramaic according to virtually every scholar that has studied it. Kharosthi also does not distinguish between long and short vowels, meaning that it is a simplified abugida in comparison to Brahmi, and was likely created to make a 'modern-looking' script, that looked more like Aramaic, the official script of the Persian Empire after Darius' reforms around 500 BC. Naturally, this raises the question of why two different, and radically different scripts were both developed from Aramaic in Pakistan under Persian rule. Logically, one of them wasn't, and since we have discovered Brahmi carvings predating Darius, we can now state categorically that Brahmi predated Kharosthi, likely by many centuries, as it would have taken time to develop.

Unlike Brahmi, Kharosthi does not appear to have been used extensively in the south, where the Tamils continued to use Tamil Brahmi script until the 5th century AD, which has also been found scattered throughout the regions they traded with, ranging from Egypt to Thailand. It is equally possible that the Brahmi script developed in southern India or Sri Lanka, and was later adopted by the Northern Indians, or, that it was already in use in Northern India long before the Persians occupied Pakistan. Unfortunately, this debate is largely dominated by national and ethic arguments, as there is no clear evidence supporting either option at this time. Regardless, it is a complex system and must have been in development long before the 'final' versions of it that appear at the beginning of recorded history across South Asia. Someone must have been writing something phonetically complex in order to need a script like this.

Few documents are complex enough to need so many specific sounds, however, the Vedas are one such collection of documents. The various forms of Sanskrit that evolved over the millennia are only known today because they were written down in the classic era in Brahmi and Kharosthi, two scripts capable of showing the differences in pronunciation that different texts were compiled in. If they were written using the Greek or Latin alphabets all of this complexity would have been lost, and we would assume they were written shortly before the time of Siddhartha. This issue of the limits of scripts to record the progress of dialects makes most proto-historic era text impossible to date. Consider for example Sanchuniathon of Beirut, who was, according to his ancient Greek biographers a Phoenician scholar that lived sometime before the Battle of Troy, circa 1200 BC. He apparently wrote a history of the Phoenicians, and a history of the Jews, neither of which survive to the present. His works were translated into Greek by Philo of Byblos in the 1st century AD, whose works also do not survive. What survives are a few quotes of Philo's translation in Eusebius' Praeparatio Evangelica, written circa 313 AD. Assuming Sanchuniathon actually lived and wrote the works attributed to him, and Philo translated his works accurately, and Eusebius quoted them accurately, how, after at least one translation, assuming one were able to read Praeparatio Evangelica in Greek, and with most of Sanchuniathon's texts missing, could one know when he lived, based on his dialect?

Furthermore, there is no reason to believe either Philo or Eusebius were treating Sanchuniathon fairly, as both were quoting him to push their own religious agendas. Compounding this is the fact that Sanchuniathon claimed his information on earliest history was translated into Phoenician from the pillars in the Temple of Amun, which would themselves date back to at least the 11th Dynasty of Egypt, circa 3502 to 3459 BC ULT (2061 to 1991 BC CET) during the Middle Kingdom, and therefore there was at least one more layer of translation that has been lost before one even read Sanchuniathon's original work. In the early Christian era after Eusebius, Sanchuniathon was often dismissed as a fool or even a hoax by Philo, and as a result, Philo's works weren't copied, and once the papyrus they were written on had deteriorated, they were lost. One of the primary points Christians used to discredit him was that his early era of the gods was so similar to Hesiod's, which they assumed he was plagiarizing, and Hesiod had lived around 700 BC, so how could Sanchuniathon have plagiarized him over 500 years earlier. In all fairness, the same could be said of the original Greek translation of the Torah, which has most of the same gods in it as Hesiod, so: did Moses plagiarize Hesiod too? or was it the Rabbis at the Library of Alexandria? or did Hesiod maybe not invent the story but simply tell one version of a very old tale?

Interest in Sanchuniathon resurfaced during the enlightenment, however, with no evidence supporting his existence he was more of a historical question mark. Archaeology of the 1900s seems to have vindicated him though, as excavations in Ugarit (near modern Latakia in Syria) have confirmed the Phoenicians or their ancestors had worshiped the same collection of gods that Sanchuniathon described since at least 1800 BC, and trading with Egypt since at least the Middle Kingdom when Amun was the dominant god. While this is not itself evidence for the existence of Sanchuniathon, it is evidence that some intermediary had existed between the ancient Phoenicians and Philo, and therefore Sanchuniathon's existence is considered likely by most historians.

Two ancient civilizations left us enough translatable texts, over a long enough period of time to observe multiple dialect shifts, similar to that which is observed in Sanskrit and Avestan: Egypt, and Mesopotamia. In Egypt, the Old, Middle, and New Kingdoms each had a distinct dialect of Egyptian, although it is harder to detect than with the Indo-Iranian languages as Hieroglyphs and Hieratic do not convey the exact sounds of the language like the abugidas of Southern Asia. In Mesopotamia, a string of Semitic languages and dialects existed: Akkadian, Old Babylonian, and Neo-Babylonian in the south, and Akkadian, Old Assyrian, and Neo-Assyrian in the north. Both Old Babylonian and Old Assyrian were regional dialects of Akkadian but emerged as separate languages circa 3350 BC ULT (1800 BC CMT).

Using the better understood Egyptian timeline as a metric, consider that there was 1443 (ULT) or 625 (CET) years between the emergence of the Old and Middle Kingdoms, and then 1922 (ULT) or 512 (CET) years between the emergence of the Middle and New Kingdoms. Therefore, there were either 3365 or 1137 years, depending on the timeline used for the transition from Old through Middle to Late Egyptian. That was simply two dialects, and even the most conservative timeline Egyptologists can imagine gives over 1100 years, and according to the ancient Egyptians was over 3300 years. Sanskrit went through five or six of these shifts, depending on one's interpretation of the two Rigvedic dialects, before the shift to Classical Sanskrit, with should have happened by 500 BC at the latest.

This means that the time when the Old-Rigvedic texts were composed should have been 2 to 3 time the lengths of the dialects shifts in Egypt, in other words somewhere between the very broad range of 10,600 and 2800 BC, but certainly not after 1500 BC when the Mitanni were invading the Middle East according to the conventional Mesopotamian timeline. Adding the Avestan dialects to the timeline as precursors to Sanskrit as most linguists agree on, would add another two or three dialects to the timeline since the life of Zoroaster, placing him anywhere between 14,000 and 3900 BC, but certainly not 50 years before Aristotle, who himself reported Zoroaster having lived between 7200 and 7300 BC. Does anyone actually believe the 'father of logic' was that stupid?

Clearly, evolutionary-linguistics is not an exact science, as demonstrated by the preceding wide range of possible points in time, nevertheless, the minimum plausible dates, using the already impossibly short conventional timelines already show that Sanskrit and Avestan must be much older than many historians are willing to consider. These purely linguistic estimates show that if anything the framework of Indo-Iranian cultures proposed in this work may be too conservative, and much older cultures were the sources of these texts, however, if there were older cultures using horses, we have yet to find their remains, moreover, the estimated time period of the use of Old-Avestan at approximately the same time that the ancients reported that Zoroaster lived seems to confirm this framework as at least more historically valid than the existing system being taught.

Nevertheless, Brahmi appears fully formed in the oldest rock-carvings it is found in, and while it must have had a developmental phase, this phase is entirely missing from the ruins we have found to date. Logically, either Brahmi is derived from another, older script, or it evolved completely independently, in which case we would expect to find a pictographic ancestor script as we have found in other regions where scripts evolved independently. This missing pictographic script could be missing because it was only ever used to write on something that deteriorates quickly, like palm leaves, however, it could also be missing from the records because it has simply been ignored.

As the Greek and Roman historians recorded, the Indians had a list of 154 kings preceding Alexander going back to the time of Rama, circa 6600 BC, it is logical to assume this would have been written down, and one of the earliest documents to have been written down. If it was a king list of north Indian kings from 6600 BC onward, then in either the CHT or ULT, it would date back to the Mehrgarh civilization and would likely have been written in the Indus script, also called Harappan script, which has been proven to actually predate the Indus Valley Civilization in the CHT, dating back to the Mature Mehrgarh Phase. The script appears late in the mature Mehrgarh phase, circa 3500 BC CHT, meaning in either timeline it was over 1500 years after the recorded life of Rama. Of course, the oldest surviving examples cannot be assumed to be the very first attempts to write something down, and only a small sample of Indus Script can be assumed to have survived to the present. Nevertheless, the remnants of the Indus script that survive to the present only become common in the Mature Harappan phase between 4150 and 3450 BC ULT (2600 and 1900 BC CHT). The Indus script disappeared abruptly at the end of the mature phase of the Indus civilization, circa 3446 BC ULT (1900 BC CHT).

The sudden disappearance of the script is strange as the civilization itself did not suddenly disappear, the implication is that they had switched to writing on a new medium such as palm leaves or copper plates. There is of course the evidence found within the Harappan ruins themselves that the Harappans were using a medium like papyrus or parchment to write on, the seals. Seals are used to seal documents with wax, these documents have always been scrolls, in every known civilization that used seals, and therefore it is a natural conclusion that the Harappans were using some kind of papyrus-like medium.

A few pieces of pottery do survive from later periods that have similar symbols to them which have been dated to as late as 1528 BC using thermoluminescence dating,[49] which implies the script was still in use 2000 years after the end of the mature phase, and around a 1000 years before the appearance of Brahmi script. Another late inscription of the Indus script was found in southern India dating to the early 2nd-millennium BC,[50] indicating that the script was used in at least two regions were the Brahmi script would later emerge.

The earliest Brahmi scripts that survive to the present are rock carvings and graffiti, neither of which is the true measure of a society. In later periods it is known that the Indians were writing on palm leaves, which deteriorate quickly but are cheap and plentiful, making them an excellent medium for most documents. Documents that were intended to survive for a long time were engraved in copper, unfortunately, these plates would have been melted down by anyone that stole them, and so would disappear quickly after the collapse of any kingdom. If either medium was in use from the Harappan Late Phase, then it would have allowed the Indus script to evolved into the Brahmi script without leaving a

---

[49]S. M. Sullivan (2011) *Indus Script Dictionary*, page viii
[50]T. S. Subramanian (2006) "Significance of Mayiladuthurai find" in *The Hindu*, May 1, 2006

trace. In either event, the Brahmi script was in use across the Indian subcontinent by 500 BC, and therefore was likely the script the ancient king list was recorded on when the Greeks arrived. If the ancient king lists, or any other ancient documents from between 3500 and 500 BC were engraved on copper plates, they have likely deteriorated by now if they weren't melted at some point, however, it is still possible that some may be found. At this time the oldest known surviving copper plate inscriptions found in India date back to the 3rd-century BC.

Dating the Harappans

Unlike in Egypt and Iraq, there has been a great deal of interest in dating the Indus Valley Civilization using scientific methods, unfortunately, the results have been so contradictory that it leaves one scratching their head. The initial timeline developed by Indologists in the 1920s was based largely on the assumption that the timeline used in Assyriology was correct, which itself was based on the timeline of Egyptian civilization popularized by James Henry Breasted around the turn of the century. Breasted had become the first American citizen to earn a degree in Egyptology, at the University of Berlin, and then wrote a series of books that tried to integrate the history of the world into the biblical timeline, specifically the Biblical timeline of the Methodist college he had started his academic career in. By the 1920s he was the head of the Oriental Institute in Chicago, which he had founded and was funded by the Rockefellers. He used the institute's wealth and influence to provided funding to Egyptologists, Assyriologists, and Indologists that supported his biblical-based timeline for world history.

Modern Egyptologists likes to ignore the fact that he was a biblical fundamentalist. His compressed timeline was developed by Biblical Historians and thoroughly debunked by Egyptologists in the 1800s, and yet by the 1920s was considered the standard timeline, even though the surviving earlier generation of Egyptologists, like Petrie, dismissed it as impossible. After that generation of Egyptologists died out the current Biblical chronology of the Conventional Egyptian Timeline became the only timeline even taught in universities, even though it is neither what the ancient Egyptians recorded, nor even possible. In the 1920s Breasted traveled extensively visiting India, Mesopotamia (British Iraq), Syria, Palestine, and Egypt, to garner supporters for his timeline. Below is a picture of Breasted (pictured left), with his team sailing from Bombay (modern Mumbai) in India to Basra in Iraq, in 1920.

The Indologists in the 1920s through 1950s that worked out the timeline of the Indus Valley Civilization were dependent on the Assyriologists that were being primarily funded by Breasted and therefore worked out a timeline for the entire civilization that spanned 3300 to 1300 BC. This timeline placed the birth of the Indus Valley Civilization in the same year that Breasted's own theories placed the birth of Egypt: 3300 BC. This civilization was immediately assumed by many Hindus to be the ruins of the ancient civilization of the epics, however, that would mean they should span a timespan of over 2 million years until at least 3100 BC, the time of Krishna.

The very small time period that the ruins are attributed never seemed right to Hindus who assumed the Indologists were allowing a western bias to shape their theories, which, of course, is correct whether the theories are correct or not, as the chronology they worked out was dependent on the timeline of Mesopotamia, who the Harappans were trading with. This has resulted in many Indians and Pakistanis wanting scientific dating as opposed to the 'hearsay' approach that the early Indologist were forced to use. In the 1960s, samples were taken from the ruins at Harappa and tested using radiocarbon dating techniques that were new at the time, and apparently confirmed the approximate dates of the Conventional Harappan Timeline, however, these samples were taken from the exposed upper levels of the ruins, and to date, no excavations of the lower levels have been possible as they are built below the waterline. This is a significant issue. Indologists claim that the civilization failed because the climate changed and the water table dropped, yet, the Indus is higher today than when Harappa was initially built, and therefore the foundation must go back to before the Indus river rose to its current level.

Between 1986 and 1996 a large number of carbon-dating tests were carried out from sites across the region which are described in western papers as confirming the CHT, however, they are still only taken from the upper exposed levels of the sites, as the water level is too high to excavate to the lower levels. Clearly, the water levels were even higher at the peak of the civilizations, as, like in Sumer, the cities were built up well above the surrounding land which must have been at least seasonally flooded. Most of the major sites in the Sind region are 12 meters (36 feet) above the surrounding land, implying that this civilization experienced significant flooding for a long period of time. Based on the fact that we have still never been able to excavate the lower levels of these cities, it seems irrational to attempt to date them at all, and the Harappan Phases of the CHT are most-likely just the tail end of this civilization, which based on the rising water levels, likely dates back well over 10,000 years.

The carbon dating that supposedly supported the CHT, did include a large number of earlier dates, so many in fact, that the CHT became untenable and was quietly changed by Indologists to 5000 BC to 1300 BC. Western history books still use the early Indologist's assumptions about the Indus Valley Civilization starting no earlier than Breasted's version of the Egyptian Civilization: 3300 BC, however Indologists no longer use these dates. Currently, the mainstream of Indology places the 'Early Food Producing Era' of the Harappan Civilization at between 6500 and 5000 BC, with the Early Harappan Phase then running to 2600 BC when the early Indologists found correlations with the Assyriologist's timeline. This chronology doesn't make a great deal of sense, as many of the earliest sites appear no less advanced than the sites of the Mature Phase, but the Mature Phase can't be moved as it is tied to the Conventional Mesopotamian Timeline.

An example of the problem in Indology is Mehrgarh, a ruin in Pakistan that was not discovered until 1974, and therefore the early Indologists did not clairvoyantly decree a date for it. Mehrgarh was a city that existed for a long time, and ran the full development process of the Indus and other civilizations, through early, mature, and late phases, which spanned approximately 5500 years. In many respects the Mehrgarh civilization was exactly the same as the rest of the Indus Valley Civilization, even sharing identical dentistry techniques, however, the carbon-dating of Mehrgarh places almost its entire history before the early Indologists claimed that the Early Harappan Phase began. The Mature Mehrgarh Phase ends at approximately 3300 BC, and the Late Mehrgarh Phase ends at approximately 2600 BC, which coincidentally, is approximately the timeline the ULT requires for the Indus Valley Civilization to have existed. It seems bizarre that anyone could believe that this completely unique civilization developed all alone and went through the entire life-cycle of the Indus Valley Civilization, but then died and the Indus Valley Civilization started from scratch and redeveloped everything identically to the Mehrgarh Civilization. Two different civilizations, where the latter inherited some of the technology of the former perhaps, but this is not the case.

The Early Harappans did not have the technology of the Late Mehrgarhans, they had the technology of the Early Mehrgarhans, who had not existed for thousands of years, and then reinvented everything exactly the same. The idea is so preposterous that Indologist adjusted the timespan of the Indus Valley

Civilization, taking it back from 3300 BC to 5000 BC to allow for this earlier Mehrgarhan technology to enter into the Early Harappan Phase, however, the two timelines still don't overlap, and now the Early Harappans are some-how getting Early Mehrgarhan technology from the Mature Mehrgarhans. While this is better, it is still not correct, it would be like a modern country only exporting 500 to 2000-year-old technology. The Mehrgarhans were no longer using those techniques, so how were they exporting them? Some of the technology can be dismissed as parallel thinking, the climate and resources are the same re-gardless of when they lived, but some of the tech-nologies are specific, like the techniques used to make fake eye-balls or to drill holes in teeth, and these cannot be dismissed as simply parallel devel-opment. These cultures were clearly around at the same time.

Other ruins have been found more recently that show this was part of a wide-scale civilization across the region, such the excavations at Bhirrana,[51] Haryana, where ruins were excavated between 2006 and 2009 that have been carbon-dated to between 7380 and 6201 BC.[52] These ruins also show what is considered 'advanced pottery' like the pottery of the Mature Indus and Mature Mehrgarh Phases, yet, again, cannot be Harappan as it is too early accord-ing to the CHT, yet, it is completely in sync with the ULT.

---

[51]Nivedita Khandekar (2012) "Indus Valley 2,000 years older than thought," *Hindustan Times*, November 4, 2012

[52]Jhimli Mukherjee Pandey (2016) "Archeologists confirm In-dian civilization is 8000 years old," *Times of India*, May 29, 2016

The Minoans

In the Mediterranean, another early culture had developed writing that also has not been deciphered yet, the Minoans as they are called today. The Minoan civilization died out before the rise of the Classical Greek civilization and was rediscovered around 1900 by a British archaeologist named Arthur Evans. He noted several parallels between Minoan and Egyptian civilization, and worked out a rough timeline of the Minoans based on the known history of Egypt, dividing the civilization into Pre-Palatial, Proto-Palatial, Neo-Palatial, and Post-Palatian periods, which roughly corresponded to the Old Kingdom, Middle Kingdom, New Kingdom, and Late Period of Egyptian history. His original work used the dates of Egyptian civilization that were universally accepted at the time, before the rise of Breasted's para-biblical timeline, and so early works listed the Minoan Civilization as beginning during the time of the Old Kingdom, around 4600 BC, as there were some huge cut-stone blocks used for building in Crete that looked like the style of cut-stone masonry of the Old Kingdom. This dating was adjusted to Breasted's para-biblical timeline once it became dominant in the mid-1900s, and so now most books incorrectly state that Evans used dates that support Breasted's timeline.

For cultures that are known to have been trading, there is surprisingly little evidence of contact until the Egyptian Middle Kingdom. The earliest Minoan artifacts have been found in northern Egypt from the reign of Amenemhat II of the 12th Dynasty, circa 3459 to 3246 BC ULT (1991 to 1803 BC CET). These artifacts are believed to date to the early Proto-Palatial period of Evan's timeline, around the same time that the Minoans began using the Linear A script. The Minoan hieroglyphs were in use earlier, by at least the late Pre-Palatial period. Neither script appears to be a direct import from either Egyptian hieroglyphs or hieratic, however, it is generally assumed both scripts were influenced by the Egyptian scripts.

There are earlier signs of contact between the Minoans and the Egyptians, such as seals found in Crete that look similar to the seals used in Egypt in the 1st Egyptian Dark Age (1st Intermediate Period), however, virtually nothing survives from that time-period, and so it is the most poorly understood period of Dynastic history. Nevertheless, the seals are considered to prove contact between the Minoans and Egyptians between 4003 to 3502 BC ULT (2900 to 2300 BC CET), in the middle of the Pre-Palatial Period of Cretan history. Earlier contact is assumed during the Old Kingdom, as the oldest stone blocks in Crete resemble the oldest stone blocks in Egypt, however, this is not considered conclusive proof of contact.

Later contact between the Minoans and other cultures are documented, such as the Minoan style frescoes discovered in ancient Canaanite ruins at Tel Kabri in Israel in 2015. The ruins of Tel Kabri where the frescoes are have been dated to the Middle Bronze era, anywhere between 2100 and 1550 BC, however, the site itself dates back as early as 6400 BC. The style of the frescoes matches the style of the late Neo-Palatial Period, and therefore is approximately the same time-period in either timeline. The dating of this entire period is hampered by the dispute between researchers in Crete and Egypt over the dating of the eruption of the Thera volcano on the island of Santorini in the Aegean sea.

The dating for the eruption of Thera has been debated for most of the last century, with a variety of views entering into the debate. The dating of the eruption is central to the dating of the late Minoan civilization, as it makes the beginning of the decline of the civilization. The volcanic eruption covered most of Crete in several meters of ash, and ash fall from Thera is recorded as far as northern Egypt. This ash is problematic as the Egyptologists decided it was circa 1500 BC, based on which dynasty the ash fell during, however, no one else seems to understand that Egyptologists know everything, and Aegean Prehistorians argued it was at least a century earlier, based on the pottery being used at the time when the eruption buried entire towns. This debate between Egyptologists and Aegean Prehistorians continued until the 1970s when early carbon-dated samples from the region confirmed the Egyptologists' view. Aegen Prehistorians rejected the carbon-dated data, insisting that it must be from circa 1650 BC, not circa 1500 BC, and in the 1990s new calibrated carbon-dating methods were used which confirmed the Aegen Prehistorians' view, which lead to the Egyptologists' rejecting the new carbon-dated data. As it stands, the best current data shows that plants buried in the ash from the eruption took place between 1627 and 1600 BC. However, this is still debated by the Egyptologists, because, if the eruption took place over a century earlier than the Conventional Egyptian Timeline states, then there is at least one century missing from the history of Egypt, and they simply don't want to re-examine the timeline again. Last time the Rockerfellers paid to have the history of Egypt changed, whose going to pay for it now?

In any event, the timeline of Crete is not significantly effected whether it is viewed on the Conventional Aegean Timeline or the Universal Long Timeline. In either timeline, most of the early Minoan history remains unknown. The Minoans appear to have been in contact with the Egyptians by the Old Kingdom, but this cannot be proven conclusively by the evidence so far found. They were using similar seals during the 1st Egyptian Dark Age, which would mean they were most likely trading by 3500 BC ULT (2300 CAT). Cretan hieroglyphs are found in the strata after 3363 BC ULT (1900 BC CAT) indicating a significant Egyptian influence by this time, and Minoan artifacts are found in Egypt confirming the trade between the cultures. This was during the Egyptian Middle Kingdom when the Egyptians dug the great canal that flooded the Fayum Depression west of modern Cairo.

This period of trade between the Egyptians and Minoans seems to have continued throughout the later periods of Minoan history, as well as trade with the Canaanite cultures in the modern states of Lebanon, Israel, and Syria. The Minoan civilization seems to have been rocked by several massive earthquakes during its existence, which were followed by massive rebuilding eras. These rebuilding eras and the changing pottery styles have led to a more developed timeline of Minoan history that divides the civilization's existence into around a dozen eras. The original era model had nine eras: Early Minoan 1, 2, and 3; Middle Minoan, 1, 2, and 3; and Late Minoan 1, 2, and 3, however, further divisions have taken place as more findings have been discovered, and now Middle Minoan 1 has an A and B era, as do others.

By the end of the Middle Minoan 2B era, Cretan hieroglyphs disappear, however, Linear A was still in use. Neither script has been deciphered, however, it is believed that they were both used for the Minoans language, like the Egyptians parallel use of hieroglyphs and hieratic. In Egypt, hieroglyphs seem to have mainly been used for religious purposes, along with anything to do with the monarchy, which was itself seen as a religious institution, while hieratic was used for more mundane things like shipping inventories, so, perhaps the situation is the same in Crete. Some proper names have been deciphered in Linear A, by comparing to Linear B, which was used to write Greek, and so we know that had some of the same gods, or at least used their names.

After the eruption of Thera, the Minoans rebuilt again, although their civilization could never recover its glory, as their cities seem to have been attacked consistently after Thera, with most showing signs of being repeatedly burnt down between whenever Thera erupted, and the ultimate disappearance of the Minoans circa 1425 BC. If the Egyptologists are right, then the Minoans rebuilt from Thera and had their cities burnt down, and then rebuilt the cities again, and then had then burnt down again, in just 75 years. Naturally, Aegean Prehistorians disagree, as using the carbon-dated timeline the Minoans had around 200 years to go through this final phase of their existence, as they were slowly conquered by the Greeks. By 1425 BC Linear A disappeared and was replaced by Linear B, which has been deciphered as early Greek, so there is no doubt that the Minoans were conquered by the Greeks, who were themselves less knowledgeable and adopted the Minoan script, as well as some of their gods.

Part 2: Mythic Era

Like the Egyptian and Sumerian texts, the ancient Sanskrit and Avestan texts include references to ancient civilizations before their own, however, in both cases, the ancients were said to have more advanced technology than one would expect. In the case of the Sanskrit epics, the current versions are believed to date to approximately 300 AD, although they are accepted as being copies of much older texts, dating to at least 500 BC, and possibly thousands of years earlier. Flying machines were common in fantasy stories from the period, appearing in the story of Icarus in Greece, Ezekiel in Judea, and Bladud in Britain, and therefore it is plausible that the airplanes were a late addition to the epics to make the enemies of the heroes seem more powerful. Emperor Ravana's massive, seven-story high, airplane is mentioned but does not play a role in the story.

Yima, Yama, Yami, and Ymir

The artificial lighting in the *Avesta* is harder to explain away, however, is sometimes dismissed as a late addition as it is in the Vendidad, which is the youngest section of the *Avesta*, written in the disputed Youngest Avestan dialect. As the origin of the Vendidad is unclear, some have dismissed the artificial lighting, and the entire story as Persian or Greek era fiction, however, the Greeks and Persians did not have artificial lighting, and it is not found in their fantasy stories, so this may be part of the original story. The story found in the *Avesta* appears to be a direct parallel of the Dumuzid saga from Sumer, and several related stories from across the world that involve the Underworld in the Mountain and the Queen of Heaven. In the Avestan version of the story, the Queen of Heaven wasn't mentioned, and King Yima the Shepherd was the focus, the parallel of King Dumuzid the Shepherd in the Sumerian story, and like the Dumuzid story, it was set over 115,000 years ago, at the onset of the current ice age.

By the Persian era he was called Jamshid, however, linguists believe the earliest version of the name is believed to have been Yemo. Both the Rigvedic Yama and the Germanic Ymir are also believed to be descended from Yemo. Both stories diverged greatly from the Avestan version. Yama, was the first man who died in the *Rig-veda*, and as a result, his name became the word meaning death, and he became the god of the dead. The Germanic version of Yemo evolved into the ice-giant Ymir, who was born in the ice rivers at the beginning of the world, and when he died there was a great flood. The

Germanic myths about Ymir appear to have only been written down in the 13th century AD, and so this story had a long time to evolve after the *Rig-veda* and Vendidad were written. Nevertheless, Ymir sounds like a personification of the ice-age itself, or at last a glacial period.

As the dialect of the Vendidad is disputed, and therefore its age is unknown, the *Rig-veda* is the oldest acknowledged text with mentions Yama along with his twin Yami. While a great deal of literature was written in later periods about them, in the *Rig-veda* Samhita there is very little. Yama was the first mortal that died and became the lord of the Underworld. His name Yama, as well as his twin's name Yami, both, translated as 'twin,' his being masculine, and hers being feminine. The nature of the two is unclear in the Vedas, as they appear as both siblings or as husband and wife depending on the text, however, it is generally believed by Hindus that they were twins in the metaphorical sense, as in identical and opposite, but not actually related. Yami later became associated with the Yamuna River, and therefore became a fertility-goddess, the opposite of Yama, the lord of the dead. This is something that can only be identified from the Classical Sanskrit period onward, and so it is unclear what their exact role was in the society of the Rigvedic Sanskrit period, however, they are found in the Old-Rigvedic sections of the *Rig-veda*, meaning they are some of the earliest people recorded in the Vedas.

In the Vendidad, the book in the *Avesta* that recounts the history of the Avestan-speaking people, tells the story of King Yima the Shepherd, however, due to disputes over the dialect, it is unclear when the book was written in relation to other Avestan and Sanskrit texts. Nevertheless, the story is strange and set before the onset of the last glacial period, or according to some interpretations, before the beginning of the current ice age. This view was discussed at length in his 1903 work 'The Arctic Homeland in the Vedas,' by Bal Gangadhar Tilak. Tilak had spent decades studying the Vedas and the *Avesta*, which he was considered a worldwide authority on. He was fluent in many languages but contemporary and ancient, and over collaborated with leading Zend and Sanskrit scholars in Britain, France, and Germany.

In 'The Arctic Homeland in the Vedas,' Tilak explored the geographic and astronomic references of the Vedas and *Avesta* and concluded that the Indo-Iranian peoples must have originated in a land in the Arctic Circle that sank into the sea between 10,000 and 8000 BC due to glacial melting, causing the Indo-Iranians to migrate south into the Eurasian continent. At the time, very little archaeological research had been done in Central Eurasia and the Steppes, however, the idea that the Indo-Iranians originated to the north was not new. The ancient Greeks recorded that the Iranian peoples lived in Ukraine, Southern Russia, and Central Asia through the Classical Era, however, there was no reference to them starting out farther north.

This idea that the Indo-Iranians stared out on a lost Arctic land was expanded to all Indo-European peoples and adopted by the Thule Society in Germany before World War 1, and then became entrenched in Nazi propaganda during World War 2,

and subsequently became unpopular among aca-
demics. In the former Soviet Union research into
Indo-Iranian origins continued incidentally, as a by-
product of the archaeological digs in the Kurgans,
and discovery of horse burials that matched the description of the setting of the *Rig-veda*. In the late
1800s Tilak's time, knowledge of the ice age was limited, and it was initially assumed the ice age had
happened suddenly trapping the mammoths of
Siberia in the ice they were found in.

The mass deaths of these mammoths is now identified as being caused by the last major cold-snap of
the most recent glacial period, today called the
Younger Dryas period, which is dated to between
10,900 and 9700 BC. Tilak dated the glacial period to
between 10,000 and 8000 BC based on the early estimates of when the ice age was believed to have been,
however, it is now recognized from several sources
that the last glacial period happened over a very
long period, beginning around 113,000 BC and ending around 9700 BC. Tilak's original research divided
the era when the *Avesta* and Vedas into several periods based on the astronomical details in the texts.

*10,000 to 8000 BC – Destruction of Arctic
homeland and initial migration south into
Eurasia.*

*8000 to 5000 BC – Pre-Orion Period – Gathic
Hymns focused on the Sun (Ahura Mazda)*

*5000 to 3000 BC – Orion Period – The vernal
equinox was in the constellation Orion. The
Hymns still contained references to the Dawn,
but now also had several references to Orion.
Tilak also identified an attempt to reform the*

ancient Aryan calendar at this time, to correct for the succession of the equinoxes.

3000 to 1400 BC – Krittika Period – The vernal equinox was in the Hindu constellation Krittika, focused on the Pleiades, which is in the Western constellation Taurus. The Vedic Hymns from this period make little sense astronomically as the composers no longer understood the astronomical basis of the original hymns.

1400 to 500 BC – Pre-Buddhist Period – The when the Sutras and associated philosophy was developed.

Tilak's astronomical interpretation of the Vedic texts has still not been challenged academically, although many do not like it for ideological reasons. It also happens to be generally in tune with the ULT, at least from the Pre-Orion period onward. Tilak's Pre-Orion period focused on the worship of the Sun and composition of the Gathic Hymns happening between 8000 and 5000 BC, corresponds roughly to the Old Avestan period of 6500 to 5500 BC, in the Bug-Dniester culture of Ukraine. Tilak's Orion Period of 5000 to 3000 BC, included most of the Rig-vedic Hymns, corresponds very closely to the Cucuteni-Trypillia and Sredny Stog culture of Romania, Moldova, and Ukraine, between 4800 and 3000 BC. Tilak did not have access to this information, as virtually no archaeological work was done in the Russian Empire, and yet, based on the astronomy, he predicted the Rig-vedic period exactly as is now known to have happened.

The story of the earlier glacial period destroying the original homeland of the Aryans is currently impossible to prove. Tilak himself did not try to set a date for it, beyond the contemporary scientific theories of the ice age, which are now known to simply be the Younger Dryas period at the end of the glacial period. Some have suggested that the story may have been set in the intermediate warm period between the Younger and Older Dryas periods when the world warmed for a few centuries. This theory holds that when the world warmed between 14,670 and 12,890 BC, humans migrated north into the newly habitable lands of northern Siberia, and when the Younger Dryas set in, they were forced south to escape the cold. While this is a valid theory, and no doubt someone ventured north into the Siberia, it is unlikely the source of this story from the Vendidad, as the Vendidad's version is the story of a warm tropical land with water snakes, being destroyed by an ice age, and a technologically advanced people surviving in an underground city, which, whether it happened or not, is not the story of primitive hunters following animals into northern Siberia.

The Vendidad clearly describes the onset of a glacial period, which destroyed the homeland of the Aryan people. This real question is not if it is the description of the onset of a glacial period, but when the Vendidad was written. The latest the text could have been written in was the Classic Era of the Persian Empire, as after that time it was in the *Avesta*, and referenced extensively in Zend commentary. Naturally, it could be discounted as a Classical period fiction, however, it seems abstractly odd that the authors would describe the onset of a glacial period as destroying their original homeland in the arctic, even if there had never been an ice age. The fact that there was a glacial period, makes the Vendidad clearly worth deeper consideration than simply dismissing it as an odd piece of fiction that somehow became entrenched in a religion with much older texts, some of which really cannot be seen as dating to much after 6000 BC, based on the linguistic evidence. The fact that the Vendidad has always been treated as an authentic Avestan test within the Zend commentary, even the earliest commentaries, means it is likely not a Persian era forgery and represents an otherwise lost Avestan dialect.

In any event, it is at least 2500 years old, yet it describes the onset of a glacial period that must have happened 110,000 years earlier. According to the story recorded in the Vendidad, before the ice age began, the Aryans lived in a tropical land with water snakes, which was then covered in snows that filled the valleys and covered the mountains. The Aryans took refuge in a subterranean town called Vara, that King Yima had built in a mountain after being fore-warned of the coming ice age by Ahura Mazda, as described in the Vendidad 2:22-30:

> 22 'And Ahura Mazda spake unto Yima, saying: 'O fair Yima, son of Vivanghat! Upon the material world the evil winters are about to fall, that shall bring the fierce, deadly frost; upon the material world the evil winters are about to fall, that shall make snow-flakes fall thick, even an aredvi [fourteen fingers] deep on the highest tops of mountains.'

> 23 'And the beasts that live in the wilderness, and those that live on the tops of the mountains, and those that live in the bosom

of the dale shall take shelter in underground abodes.'

24 *'Before that winter, the country would bear plenty of grass for cattle, before the waters had flooded it. Now after the melting of the snow, O Yima, a place wherein the footprint of a sheep may be seen will be a wonder in the world.'*

25 *'Therefore make thee a Vara, long as a riding-ground [2 miles] on every side of the square, and thither bring the seeds of sheep and oxen, of men, of dogs, of birds, and of red blazing fires. Therefore make thee a Vara, long as a riding-ground on every side of the square, to be an abode for man; a Vara, long as a riding-ground on every side of the square, for oxen and sheep.'*

26 *'There thou shalt make waters flow in a bed a hathra [1 mile] long; there thou shalt settle birds, on the green that never fades, with food that never fails. There thou shalt establish dwelling-places, consisting of a house with a balcony, a courtyard, and as gallery.'*

27 *'Thither thou shalt bring the seeds of men and women, of the greatest, best, and finest on this earth; thither thou shalt bring the seeds of every kind of cattle, of the greatest, best, and finest on this earth.'*

28 *'Thither thou shalt bring the seeds of every kind of tree, of the highest of size and sweetest of odour on this earth; thither thou shalt bring the seeds of every kind of fruit, the best of savour and sweetest of odour. All those seeds shalt thou bring, two of every kind, to be kept inexhaustible there, so long as those men shall stay in the Vara.'*

> 29 'There shall be no humpbacked, none
> bulged forward there; no impotent, no lunatic;
> no malicious, no liar; no one spiteful, none
> jealous; no one with decayed tooth, no leprous
> to be pent up, nor any of the brands wherewith
> Angra Mainyu stamps the bodies of mortals.'

> 30 'In the largest part of the place thou shalt
> make nine streets, six in the middle part, three
> in the smallest. To the streets of the largest part
> thou shalt bring a thousand seeds of men and
> women; to the streets of the middle part, six
> hundred; to the streets of the smallest part,
> three hundred. That Vara thou shalt seal up
> with thy golden seal, and thou shalt make a
> door, and a window self-shining within."

The term 'self-shining window,' has always been interpreted in Zend commentaries as some kind of magical artificial light. Today, artificial lights are no longer seen as magical, however, for thousands of years, the self-shining light was as magical as the flying machine. The Magi, who were the priests of the Zoroastrian religion, is also the source of the English word magical, as they're ancient texts apparently described how to build many magical devices before Alexander destroyed their archives. If these magical texts ever actually existed, and if they contained something other than nonsense, it's possible they were describing technology. It is generally accepted that the Baghdad Batteries were built by Magi, which would mean that they maintained a rudimentary understanding of electricity as late as 50 AD, however, what these batteries were used for is still a matter of much debate.

The batteries themselves are even debated. They were discovered in the ruins of ancient Ctesiphon, in Iraq. Ctesiphon was the capital of the ancient Parthian Empire, and therefore they are assumed to be from the Parthian era, however, no one bothered carbon-dating them, and they were plundered from National Museum of Iraq during the American-led 2003 Invasion of Iraq, so we may never know their true age unless more are unearthed. They were first proposed as batteries in 1938 by Wilhelm König, an assistant at the National Museum of Iraq. He noted several ancient Mesopotamian objects that had been plated with gold, and suggested the batteries had been used for electroplating. Various experts had chimed in during the past century, either supporting or dismissing the idea. Generally, engineers supported the idea that these are batteries, while Assyriologists dismiss the idea that these are batteries, because... you know, 'they didn't know about electricity.'

Archaeologists have yet to propose an alternative idea of what these batteries were, other than some kind of weird jar for storing papyrus. No papyrus was found in the batteries, and no jars for storing papyrus have been found anywhere else like these. What was found in the batteries was acidic residue, and the lack of acid is the only thing that stops these batteries from giving off voltage. Multiple duplicates have been created which prove they do work for small scale power generation when acids which the Parthians had access to are added, such as lemon juice, or grape juice. But, you know... 'they didn't know about electricity,' so 'they're not batteries.'

The close-minded circular logic of the cultist convicts to itself. If these aren't batteries, someone built something that just happens to work like a battery, around 2000 years ago, for unknown reasons.

The problem with interpreting these as batteries is that if they were, they did not develop into an electrical system like we have today 2000 years ago. Therefore, many reject the idea. Surely if they could build batteries, they would build hydroelectric dams and ... nuclear power plants? If in fact, all they had were batteries, they would have been of very little use. The modern electrical systems were built for lighting first and foremost. After houses were wired for lighting, other appliances that use electricity became practical. No one said, 'I've invented an electrical dishwasher, now let's build an electrical grid so I can start selling them. Without the invention of the light bulb, we most likely would still not have an electrical grid, and certainly would not have developed hydro-electric plants, nuclear technology, or the internet.

The galvanic cell, which is what the Baghdad batteries look like, was invested in the 1700s. It took a century of capitalist investment to drive the technology to the point where we were building street lighting grids for cities, and there is no reason to believe the Baghdad batteries were ever in the hands of capitalists. There was no patent office in the Parthian or Roman empires. The patent of the time was secrecy. To this day, historians aren't sure what Greek fire was, although it is widely described as a fluid that burnt virulently and was used to destroy enemy ships at sea. It has been suggested it could have been naphtha, or pigs lard, or several other things, however, we don't know, because the Greeks who created and sold it did not want anyone to know, and so they didn't write it down. If the Baghdad batteries were being used to electroplate gold onto silver or lead objects, surely whoever was doing it would not have told anyone. They were, after all, running a con, who advertised that.

This electroplating technology also explains the myth that the Magi could transmute other metals to gold, but the 'spell was broken' if the metals were melted down, and the metals would revert to their original form. This is exactly what would happen if they were electroplating other metals. If it was the Magi using these batteries, then their origin is less mysterious as if the *Avesta* is accurate, they had more advanced technologies at one point but had been wandering between nations for thousands of years. In the Vendidad, there are brief descriptions of the 15 lands they lived in after leaving the Vara. In each country, they found something that was undesirable and so left. These undesirable things included termites, cannibals, pedophiles, and atheists, and each time they moved on to another land, eventually settling in the land were Zoroaster met the beings of light, and sang the Gathas. This means before the Avestan speakers were in the Bug-Dniester region, circa 6500 to 5500 BC, they had already migrated through 15 lands. If their story of being trapped in/ on a mountain surrounded by glaciers is accurate, then they would have likely been trapped until sometime after 20,000 BC, the Last Glacial Maximum, when the glaciers were at their greatest ex-

panse. If Europe the glaciers initially retreated between 20,000 and 16,000 BC, while in Siberia the
glaciers began retreating after 15,000 years ago. In
either case, there was move than enough time to
settle for some time in 15 nations before ultimately
ending up in Ukraine by 6500 BC.

If this is, in fact, the story of an ancient civilization in the arctic being destroyed by the onset of the
last glacial period, then the original story would
have been set approximately 115,000 years ago, at
approximately the same time as the life of King Dumuzid the Shepherd in the Sumerian king lists, who
was recorded as having lived between 129,579 and
93,579 BC. The number of similarities between these
two shepherd-kings is striking, and difficult to dismiss. Both were reported to have lived in an underground community of some kind, specifically Ganzir
and the Vara, although the Dumuzid story makes
Ganzir sound more like a gulag than the Vara was in
the Yima story. Comparing the Vedic version to the
Sumerian, both Dumuzid and Yama became associated with death, and a lord of the Underworld, and
both were married to (or twins with) a fertility goddess, specifically Yami (later Yamuna) and Inanna
(later Ishtar).

While similar stories across a region are not un-
usual, as religious cults migrate between cultures
and adopt the languages of their new cultures, these
stories are hard to trace to an origin. The Sumerians
and Steppes cultures do not seem to have been in
contact. It is possible in the ULT that given enough
time, the cult of Dumuzid could have expanded as
far north as the Steppes, however, this still would

not explain the glacial period, which was not part of the Dumuzid story. In the surviving Sumerian stories the land outside the mountain Ganzir is built in becomes a wasteland, but snow, for which a word did not exist in Sumerian, was not mentioned. Conversely, in the ULT the Sumerian civilization existed before the Avestan speaking Bug-Dniester culture, and therefore the Sumerian story could not be based on the Avestan one. If one only considers the conventional timelines, then the Bug-Dniester culture did predate the Sumerians, and could have been the source of the Sumerian story, but only if one accepted that it was an Avestan culture and that Indo-Iranian culture extended south into Mesopotamia from the dawn of Sumerian civilization, which there is no other evidence of. In any event, neither the Avestan nor Sumerian languages show any traces of the other, which one would expect if the cross-fertilization happened as recently as 5000 BC ULT (3000 BC CMT).

These appear to be two separate versions of the same story, set circa 115,000 years ago. In both stories, there is machinery in the underworld which seems out of place if these were always metaphors for the state of death. In both cases, the world outside the mountain became wasteland and remained that way for a very long time. In the case of the *Avesta*, some laws had punishments of up to one thousand years, for the family of the criminal. Clearly, they weren't in the Vara for just a few years or a few decades. The laws strictly controlled the birth rate, and violators were sent to the 'worst existence,' which sounds like extradition to the wastelands outside, however, the Dumuizd saga from Sumer offers another interpretation. In the Sumerian version of the story, on the top of the mountain was the garden of the gods, where those not forced to work in Ganzir lived freely.

This is similar to the paradise that was reported to have existed on a mountain in some Zoroastrian stories, according to early Greek interpretations of Zoroastrianism. The English word paradise was adopted via the Greek word for paradise from the Avestan term for a 'walled-garden,' however, the garden on the mountain does not appear in the *Avesta*. It seems the sections dealing with it were lost when Alexander burnt the Avestan archives, however, it seems unlikely that is was a completely unrelated mountain, and many Zend scholars have accepted that there was a walled garden on top of the mountains, and likely where the people of the Vara grew their food. Some have even suggested that the original story was probably just about a walled garden being built by Yima, and not the bunker-town described in the Vendidad, however, this is simply an opinion, not based on the existence of alternate versions of the story within the *Avesta*. If the Paradise was built on the top of the mountain the Vara was in, like the Garden of the Gods above Ganzir, then the 'worst existence' may have been working in the Vara, as life in Ganzir was described.

Nevertheless, while Neanderthal remains have been found north of the Arctic circle from the time period in question, so far no modern human remains have been found. Of course, as the ground is generally frozen year-round, and there is a general assumption that little or nothing will be found, there continues to be little archaeological research done in northern Russia.

The Rama Epics

Several Classical Sanskrit epics are set in the ancient Indus Valley Civilization, most notably, the *Mahabharata* and the *Ramayana*. The idea that Krishna was a Harappan has been generally accepted by Hindus since the civilization was discovered in the 1920s, as he lived in both the region and era of civilization. Hindus expected to find the ruins of a civilization in the region that dated from that time, and therefore there it was not surprising, however, Indologists are cautious about ascribing the *Mahabharata* to this civilization. There are a large number of similarities between the Harappan ruins and the described civilization in the *Mahabharata*, for instance, both civilizations appear to be river-based, using boats to carry the majority of their cargo.

Before the domestication of horses by the steppes peoples, the majority of cargo and transportation seems to have been done by boat, and as a result, almost all early civilizations were based along rivers of lakes. In India though, there was a beast of burden being used, the elephant. Asian elephants are more docile than their African cousins and have been used throughout recorded history as a beast of burden, as well as a war-machine. Armored elephants are reported as being what stopped Alexander the Great's invasion of India. In the *Mahabharata*, both cattle and elephants are being used, however in minor roles. The major animal being used is the horse, which the Harappans did not have. Not only are there no remains of horses found in the ruins of the civilization, it is difficult to imagine their usefulness as a means of transportation between cities surrounded by water. If the Harappans had horses, they no doubt would have built their civilization very differently, with roads crossing the dry inland regions of the subcontinent, instead, we find they built their cities in flood plains. If anything, the introduction of the horse to their civilization would have lead to such a transition that it could be interpreted by later archaeologists as a collapse, as the people would have suddenly had access to a much greater range of territory, and would have abandoned their flooded cities.

It is the existence of these horses that causes the authenticity of the *Mahabharata* to be questioned, however, there is no reason to assume these were part of the original story. If the *Mahabharata* was a Harappan story, then it was written or recited in the ancient language of the Harappans for thousands of years before the arrival of the Indo-Aryans. As it appears to have only been translated into Sanskrit during the Classical era, circa 500 BC, it is fair to assume that the horses would have been inserted into the story at that time. The *Mahabharata* is not intended to describe a group of primitive barbarians bashing each other with clubs, it is the backdrop for the Bhagavad Gita, what would have been viewed as the greatest philosophical doctrine by the scribes that took the time to translate it into Sanskrit. They likely described the ancient land with the same technologies they were familiar with so the reader would understand what was happening. These anachronistic horses would have been much like Shakespeare giving Caesar a clock, or writing that Cleopatra wanted to play billiards, things people in the 1700s would have understood, but not historically accurate.

The dating of the *Ramayana* is more problematic, as, while it is set in the region of the later Indus Valley Civilization, its dating has been debated for over a thousand years. The earliest non-Indian records of Rama, the Greek records of Indian-Dionysus and Roman records of Indian-Bacchus, both place his life circa 6600 BC, which places it before the Harappan 1 Phase in either the CHT or ULT. Naturally, with the ruins near Bhirrana carbon-dated to between 7380 and 6201 BC, both timelines will need to be updated, and to Rama's existence circa 6600 BC becomes an archaeological possibility. However, Hindus do generally not believe Rama lived around 6600 BC, instead they date his life to millions of years earlier. Conversely, Indologists that consider the *Ramayana* as being based on a real story that became mythologized generally suggest he lived maybe around 1200 BC, at that 'Mediterranean Iron Age' date that seems to underpin all of Indology.

Another aspect of the Rama story that results in people generally dismissing it as a fairy-tale is the existence of a large island called Lanka, which is simply the Sanskrit word for 'island.' This is not generally considered Sri Lanka, as is was described as being 1300 kilometers (100 yojanas) from India. This would place it either in the Indian Ocean, south of the equator, East Africa, or Indonesia. Hindu commentary has generally treated it as a sunken continent since the 1700s, however, it is most likely a reference to the islands of Indonesia, as it is described as one of many large islands, one being 800 miles across. The following is the description of India and Lanka from *Ramayana* when Rama sent Hanuman to look for Sita:

"To search for Sita in the southern region, Sugriva hand-picked the best of the vanaras. Nila son of Agni, Hanuman the son of Vayu, the supremely mighty Jambavan, and many other mighty vanaras were chosen to constitute this party. He appointed Angada, the son of Vali, and the prince regent himself as the commander of the vanara forces that constituted this search party.

In his briefing, Sugriva specially mentioned those places which were difficult of access. He said: 'Start with the Vindhya mountains, and the plains of the rivers Narmada, Krishna Godavari, and Varada. Thoroughly search the regions of Mekhala, Utkala, Vidarbha, Vanga, Kalinga, Andhra, Cola, Pandya, and Kerala. Then proceed to the Malaya mountains, with the blessings of the sage Agastya whom you will see there.

Proceed from there to the golden gate city of the Pandyas whose city walls are studded with precious stones. Between the city and the hermitage of Agastya is the Mahendra mountain which is full of gold, and which Agastya sank into the ocean. Indra himself visits this mountain every fortnight.

Beyond this is the inaccessible island which is eight hundred miles wide: it is inaccessible to human beings. Search this island carefully. Surely that is the territory of the powerful Ravana who deserves to be killed. Before you leave that territory make sure that Sita is not there: do not leave anything in doubt.

> *Eight hundred miles beyond that island in the ocean is the partly submerged island Puspitaka with its high mountains resembling gold and silver. One hundred and twelve miles beyond Puspitaka is the mountain Suryavan, beyond that Vaidytua, and beyond that the mountain Kunjara where the sage Agastya has a hermitage which is eighty miles broad, and eighty miles high, made of gold and precious gems. There exists the abode of nagas known as Bhogavati. Search this dreadful place carefully. Search the mountain beyond this, known as Risabha.*

> *Beyond that is the world of the Manes: do not go there. Wherever you go search for Sita carefully. Whoever returns first in a month and says Sita has been discovered will enjoy luxuries equal to mine, for he will be most dear to me.'"*

This description cannot be applied to Eastern Africa, or anything directly south of India, including the submerged plateaus near Madagascar, however, does apply to the islands of Southeast Asia. If this is a description of ancient Malaysia and Indonesia, then there should be ruins in the region that date to the period, and there are. At Gunung Padang, on the island of Java, is a megalithic site that has been carbon-dated to between 10,500 BC and 2800 BC. Only the top 10 meters have been excavated, and the site is known to go down to at least 15 meters, which researchers at the site have estimated could be 20,000 years old. The earlier dates are speculation, however, the upper levels do prove the site existed at the time of Ravena's apparent kingdom in the region. The site is extensive, covering an estimated 25 hectares (62 acres), and the east side has an estimated 100 stone terraces.[53]

Unfortunately, the historical accuracy of the *Ramayana* is very doubtful regardless of when it happened. It is a story with talking monkeys, talking bears, ancient airplanes, ancient horses in India, and what sounds like extra-terrestrials orbiting the Earth, Moon, and Sun in massive flying cities. Naturally, there has been little real interest in trying to determine when it happened by western Indologists, and Hindu Indologists are often guided by their religious beliefs, which generally point to millions of years ago, and therefore, nothing found to date in India or Pakistan would date to the correct time period. Research into the *Ramayana* is further ham-

[53]Zulhidayat Siregar (June 28, 2012) "Tim Terpadu Riset Mandiri: Gunung Padang Truly Extraordinary," *Kantor Berita Politik RMOL*

pered by the fact that there are dozens of different versions spread throughout South and Southeast Asia, and they are different. Each version of the story has the same central conflict between Rama and Ravana, however, Rama isn't always the hero, sometimes its Hanuman, the talking monkey, or sometimes even Ravana, Rama's enemy. In the Hanuman focused versions, he generally ends up married to a mermaid, who is sometimes Ravana's daughter. While it is a natural assumption that all versions of this story must descend from an original, this is not something that can be shown through any literary analysis, and in fact, each version seems as authentically ancient as any other. In the Philippines, even non-literate tribes have been shown to have a local version of the Rama epic.[54] Some major versions include:

Ramayana: Indo-Aryan version of northern India

Ramavataram: Tamil (Dravidian) version of southern India

Ranganatha Ramayanam: Telugu (Dravidian) version of southern India

Torave Ramayana: Kannada (Dravidian) version of southern India

Yama Zatdaw: Burmese version

Ramakien: Thai version

Phra Lak Phra Lam: Laotian version

Reamker: Cambodian version

Hikayat Seri Rama: Malaysian version

[54]E. Arsenio Manuel (1963) "A Survey of Philippine Folk Epics," *Asian Folklore Studies*, Volume 22, Pages 1-76

Ramakavaca: Balinese version of Indonesia

Maharadia Lawana: Maranao version of the Philippines[55]

Lam-Ang: Ilocano version of the Philippines

---

[55]Mellie Leandicho Lopez (2008) *A Handbook of Philippine Folklore*

Rama and Ra

All of the varying versions of the Rama epic point to the core of the story being very old, much older than 1200 BC. There are also several striking parallels between the various versions of the Rama epic and the cult of Ra in the earliest phase of Egyptian history. Ra later became the Sun-god during the Middle Kingdom through his association with Amun, and again in the New Kingdom through his association with Atum, the Sun, as all of their cult centers were in On, later called Heliopolis by the Greeks. During the New Kingdom and then Late Period On (Heliopolis) rose to religious dominance as the center of Sun-worship in Egypt. This was the time when Sun-gods rose to prominence in the Middle East, and at one point included the Zoroastrian and Jewish Gods, before they began to diverge again.

However, thousands of years earlier Ra was not the Sun-god, but instead the central character in the early dynastic struggle between Ra and Apophis, a snake-god. In the earliest surviving texts from the 2nd dynasty, he was aided in his fight against Apophis by Set and Babi, a story that later became absorbed into the solar cult that developed. Ra was in ancient times called the King of the Three Worlds, the same title given to Ravana in many versions of the Rama epic. Several other animal-deities are also shared between the *Ramayana* variations as well as other early Sanskrit epics, and the earliest Egyptian and Sumerian religions, which support the idea that these are interconnected religions.

These animal-human icons are often disregarded as deified animal totems, however, this simple dismissal of the icon results in ignoring the existence of a widespread belief system in early times. If Hinduism had have died out a thousand years ago, and its statures and artwork were examined through the same lens, it would simply be dismissed as a bunch of deified animal totems, and there would be no reference to anything like Hinduism in modern scholarly work. Fortunately, it did not, and not only maintained some of the world's oldest literature, the Vedic Texts, but also a rich religion that is replete animalistic iconography. Hindus believe that the spirit can incarnate as animals or humans, and perhaps, this is a better lens through which to view the ancient animal-human icons. Regardless of the source of these icons, a large number of people, believed something, for a very long time, and it is the fact that they believed it that is important from a historical perspective, not whether the belief was valid from our perspective. This idea that it was simply primitive non-sense was used to dismiss it by early Christian scholars and is now also used by their atheist descendants.

The Monkey-God

Babi was Ra's main ally in the early Egyptian stories and was in every respect identical to Hanuman. In the past couple of centuries, several Orientalists and then Indologists have proposed that Hanuman was a Harappan deity, based on the etymology of his name. The orientalist F. E. Pargiter theorized that Hanuman was an early-Dravidian deity, and the name 'Hanuman' was a Sanskritization of the Old Tamil words *Aan-mandhi* meaning 'male monkey.' The Hindu scholar Ray Govindchandra influenced by Pargiter's opinion, suggested in 1976 that the early Indo-Aryans may have invented a Sanskrit etymology for the deity's name after they accepted Hanuman into their pantheon.[56] On the next page are two pictures, the left is an ancient Egyptian carving of Babi, and to the right is a traditional depiction of Hanuman.

The Egyptian name 'Babi,' translates as 'bull of the baboons,' and roughly means 'alpha-male of the baboons.'[57] There are several identical attributes to these gods. They both were always depicted as carrying a mace, and both were reported as flying in machines of some kind during the respective battles they fought in. Ra's flying machine was described as a flying barge in Egyptian records, while Ravana's flying machine was simply called an airplane (vimana). Ancient statues of Hanuman are found throughout Southeast Asia, where Hindu-based be-

---

[56]Philip Lutgendorf (2007) *Hanuman's Tale: The Messages of a Divine Monkey*. Page 40
[57]George Hart (2005) *The Routledge Dictionary of Egyptian Gods and Goddesses*, Second Edition, Page 44

liefs were common before Islam spread into the region.

Statues of a monkey-god, or monkey-people, have also been found in the region around Gimpie, Queensland, Australia, which cannot be a local development, as monkeys are not indigenous to Australia. Monkey-gods with identical iconography to Hanuman and Babi have been found in Mayan ruins in Copán, Honduras, pictured below. At the time of contact, the Spanish explorers recorded that in the Alta Verapaz region, the monkey-gods were known as *Hun-Ahan*, and *Hun-Chevan*, which is translated as *Hun-Chowen* today in the Popol Vuh. The similarity of the names and iconography seems more than just coincidental and may indicate a trans-Pacific spread of an early Hindu belief system. Copán was the capital city of a major Mayan kingdom between 426 and 822 AD,[58] believed to have been known as Oxwitik at the time. It is unclear when Copán was originally settled, however, the settlement dates back to the Early Preclassic period, between 2500 and 1500 BC.

---

[58]Robert J. Sharer and Loa P. Traxler (2006) *The Ancient Maya* (6th edition), Page 333.

The Sha and the Enusha

The other major ally of Ra was Set, a strange-looking god, who was depicted either as a Set-headed human, or a Set-creature. Like other Egyptian gods, he was depicted either as an animal or as a human-animal hybrid, however, in the case of Set the animal is unknown. This creature was depicted in a tomb from the Naqada I phase of Egyptian pre-history, which in the ULT would date to between 6500 and 6000 BC, approximately 500 to 1000 years before the foundation of the 1st dynasty circa 5510 BC ULT.

A photograph of Set and Nephthys from circa 1250 BC.

It was subsequently depicted on the mace of the King Scorpion shortly before the foundation of the 1st dynasty, meaning this creature was clearly considered important around the time of the foundation of Egypt. The Egyptian name for the creature was Sha, which may have been an earlier name for Set.

A photo of a carving of Varaha from Mahabalipuram in Tamil Nadu, from the 7th-century.

In India, a similarly named mysterious creature was also associated with the Rama story: Emusha, whose name was later changed to Varaha in the Sanskrit epics. Varaha means pig or boar in Sanskrit, and as a result, Varaha is depicted as a boar-headed human in Hindu art, however, it is unclear what Enusha originally looked like. In some of the later pyramid texts

Set, was depicted as a boar, meaning that there must have been some cross-fertilization between the later Egyptian and early-Hindu religions.

This also suggests that the earliest Egyptian version of the Ra story was another of the many renditions of the Rama story, however, this would place its origin before the Old Kingdom in Egypt, circa 4945 BC ULT, and likely before the oldest known depictions of a Sha from between 6500 and 6000 BC ULT. This dating would support the ancient Greek and Roman claims about the ancient Indian king lists which recorded Rama as ruling circa 6600 BC, however, it also means that the Hanuman and Emusha creatures were part of the story from its earliest versions.

The Werelions and Werejaguars

Narasimha is a werelion within the Vaishnavism branch of Hinduism, created by Vishnu so he could incarnate on the Earth. Narasimha was also known as the Great Protector as he incarnated on Earth to protect humanity. His name means 'lion-man' in Sanskrit however he was not found in the Vedas, which implies he was a Harappan god adopted by the Indo-Aryans after they arrived in South Asia. In Egypt, Bastet and Sekhmet were two virtually identical goddesses, one from Upper Egypt, and one from Lower Egypt, which were venerated since at least the 2nd dynasty. Both are believed to have been pre-dynastic, and likely local versions of the same early goddess as Upper and Lower Egypt spoke different languages and were separate nations before being unified circa 5510 BC ULT. To the south in Nubia, a virtually identical male lion-man god was known as Adepemek. Below are two photos, a photo of two Narasimhas at a temple in India to the left, and a photo of an ancient Egyptian carving of Bastet and Sekhmet to the right.

Bastet and Sekhmet ultimately became sisters in the Egyptian religion, the two protectors of Ra, and Adepemak was sometimes called their brother. In the Egyptian story, the werelions hunted and ultimately killed Apophis, the enemy of Ra, who was depicted by the Middle Kingdom as a giant-serpent that wanted to eat Ra, the Sun. Meanwhile in the early-Hindu story Narasimha, he incarnated on the Earth to stop a group of Nagas, which were snake-men, from stealing the Sun. Obviously, the stories sound like nonsense, but they are the same story, one in Ancient Egypt, likely dating to the pre-dynastic era, and the other in India, likely dating to the Indus Valley Civilization.

In Mesopotamia, these creatures were called Ugallu from at least the Old Babylonian and Old Assyrian eras through the ends of the Neo-Assyrian and Neo-Babylonian Empires. The name itself is Akkadian, meaning 'big day,' which indicates the being originated in the Akkadian civilization at the latest, however, he was generally associated with the Sumerian demon Lulal, the younger son of Inanna, which Ugallu back to Inanna's early husband Zababa, whose iconography included lions. As the Egyptian, Harappan, and Mesopotamian cultures were trading from the pre-Dynastic era of Egyptian history, it's possible the werelions of Egypt could have been adopted by the Mesopotamians and Indians at any point, if they originated in Egypt.

In ruins of the Olmec civilization of southern Mexico which have been dated to between 1600 to 1200 BC, multiple carvings of werejaguars have been found which are similar looking to the werelions of

Eurasia, but are generally dismissed as a local development independent of what was happening in Eurasia. While this is possible, combined with the large number of other parallels found between Eurasian and Mesoamerican cultures, these werejaguar figures point to being part of a larger pattern of religious iconography that existed across the ancient world in the 2nd millennium BC.

Two Ugallu warriors, left, and an Olmec werejaguar figurine, right.

The Bird-Man

Garuda is the eagle-man god of the epics. His Vedic equivalent was Syena, and the two are generally seen as being the same god by Hindus. Syena is simply the Sanskrit word for 'eagle,' and therefore he is seen as being an eagle-god, however, the Vedas did not specify if this was simply an eagle or the eagles that were being worshiped, or an eagle-man-god, so the concept that Syena was an eagle-man-god could be an anachronism, and they may have simply been prayers to regular eagles in the Vedas. Garuda is believed to be derived from the Early Dravidian (or Old Tamil) word 'karug-u' meaning 'eagle,'[59] however, Garuda has always been depicted as being a bird-man hybrid, like Horus in Egypt, whose name literally translates as 'falcon.'

In Egypt, the earliest representations of Horus depict him as a falcon, however, he became anthropomorphized over the course of the civilization. These three deities could be dismissed as three random animal-totems that became deified at the beginning of civilization, however, their stories are intertwined with the Ra-Rama story, and therefore cannot simply be ignored. In early Egyptian stories of Ra, he was the father of Horus through Isis, however, in other early texts, this was Horus the Elder. In either case, he was later replaced by Osiris by the New Kingdom.

---

[59]Robert Caldwell (1996) *A Comparative Grammar of the Dravidian or South-Indian Family of Languages*, Third Edition, Page 591

Two photographs showing the evolution of Horus in Egypt. The Narmer Palette from the beginning of the 1st Dynasty, circa 5510 BC ULT (3100 BC CET) to the left, and a carving of Horus from the Greek era, between 330 and 30 BC to the right. Below is a photo of a Balinese carving of Garuda fighting nagas, showing the common iconography with Chinese water-dragons (left), and a traditional Indian interpretation (right).

In Hinduism, Garuda is not associated with Rama, however, the main focus of his story is the war against the nagas, like Narasimha. The Hindu story of Garuda fighting the nagas is well documented throughout Southeast Asia, as the region was home to many Hindu temples before the arrival of Islam.

The Hindu story of Garuda fighting the nagas almost identical to the Sumerian story of the Anzu Bird fighting the snakes. The Anzu Bird was not depicted as a bird-man, but rather an ostrich or stork-like being, like the Bennu Bird in Egypt. The story of Lugal Banda and the Anzi Bird was set much earlier according to the Sumerian king list, circa 9124 BC ULT, which implies the story itself is much older than Rama but became merged with the Ra story in Egypt. Nevertheless, the iconography of the war against the nagas continued into the later epics, with the naga Ulupi fighting alongside Rama in the *Ramayana*, and Krishna defeating the naga Kaliya in the *Mahabharata*.

In the Assyrian Old Kingdom, the bird-man showed up as a replacement for the aquatic Abgal of earlier Mesopotamian civilizations, becoming the teachers of humanity. In the ULT this civilization existed between circa 3278 to 2965 BC, while in the conventional Mesopotamian timeline it existed between 1905 and 1517 BC. These bird-men continued through later eras of Assyrian civilization, not as gods, but as teachers and messengers from the gods. Below is an Assyrian seal from the Assyrian Middle Kingdom circa 1200 BC. These messengers passed into the later Middle Eastern religions, becoming the Jewish, Christian, and Islamic angels.

The Snake-People

The nagas and similar snake people appear in most of the Asian religions and are often aquatic. In the Indian epics, they are land-living snake-people, who were both described as enemies and allies of the heroes. They are described as living in tribes and kingdoms that are virtually identical to the human tribes and kingdoms, with equivalent weapons and technology. In the Southeast Asian versions of the Rama epic, such as the Thai *Ramakien* and Cambodian *Reamker*, the nagas were replaced by mermaids. In the Southeast Asian versions of the saga, Rama also wasn't always the focus of the story, sometimes it was focused on Rama's brother Laksmana, or Hanuman. In the Cambodian *Reamker*, there was a large focus on Hanuman and Sovann Maccha, the mermaid daughter of Ravana.

These mermaids of Southeast Asian versions of the Rama epic were often described as water-dragons, not giant dragons, like their western mythological cousins, but human-sized water-dragons, a type of aquatic-reptilian-people. These water-dragons also appeared in the foundational myths of China as Fuxi and Nuwa, a brother and sister pair of water-dragons that either created humanity or taught humanity the arts of civilization, depending on the specific myth. Similar creatures were reported in Egypt, Greece, and Sumer, in each myth being amphibious teachers. In the Greek period of Egyptian history, Isis and Osiris were depicted almost identically to Fuxi and Nuwa, however, similar stories about them being teachers of civilization go back to the New Kingdom. In early Greek mythology, Cercrops was an identical amphibious teacher of civilization, and in Sumeria, there were several amphibious teachers, called Abgals, the most famous and iconic being Oannes.

A photograph of a mural depicting Hanuman and Sovann Maccha at Wat Phra Kaew, in Bangkok.

This mythical war seems to have ultimately been lost by the water-dragons as the bird-people ultimately became the dominant set of gods in most cultures, later being demoted to angels in the west, while in most cultures mermaids and dragons were demoted all the way to fiction. This story of a group of snake-teachers being overthrown bird-men became the backdrop of Judaism, Christianity, and Islam, so this story, whatever it was originally about, seems to still be happening in the pan-human psyche.

The Elephant-Man

Another odd creature that shows up in Hindu iconography is Ganesha, who has a variety of local names throughout South and Southeast Asia. Throughout the region, he had always been depicted as a human-sized elephant-headed man. Again, there are elephants in India, and so it is not difficult to see this being developing from an animal-totem, as is generally assumed by non-Hindus, however, there are specific aspects of this story that try it into the epics. The *Mahabharata* was apparently written down by Ganesha as Vyasa dictated it, placing Ganesha, at least figuratively, in the Harappan civilization.

Pictures of the Oxford Palette from circa 5510 BC ULT, left, one of the earliest surviving representations of Ganesha circa 500 AD, center, and a Ganesha-like statue discovered in Australia in 1906. The Ganesha-like creature in the Oxford Palette in the lower-left area, left of the giraffe.

The elephant-headed man himself, is something that generally does not appear outside of South and Southeast Asia, the range of the Asian elephants, however, is depicted on the Oxford Palette, a caved stone tablet from the beginning of the dynastic history in Egypt, circa 5500 BC ULT. The Egyptians did not have elephants, or elephant-headed gods, so who was this carving representing? The creature arguably does not look like an elephant, however, it does have a trunk, which only elephants have, and therefore does seem like an attempt to depicts one, by someone that had never seen one.

The name Ganesha is another important factor, as it formed by combining the Sanskrit words *gana* meaning group, and *isha* meaning lord.[60] In this context, the group is the Ganas, a group of phantoms or spirits that attend Shiva.[61] This means that the name Ganesha is not whatever he was called by the ancient Harappans, but an Indo-Aryan translation. If the original name was translated accurately into Sanskrit, then is had an identical meaning to the Sumerian Enlil, which translates from Sumerian as 'Lord of Phantoms.'[62] Enlil, later called Ellil by the Akkadians and Babylonians was never depicted as far as we know, and so it is unclear if he was also elephant-headed.

---

[60] A. K. Narain (1991) "Gaṇeśa: A Protohistory of the Idea and the Icon" in Robert Brown, editor: *Ganesh: Studies of an Asian God*, Page 21-22

[61] Anna L. Dallapiccola (2002) *Dictionary of Hindu Lore and Legend*

[62] P. Michalowski (1989) "The Lamentation over the Destruction of Sumer and Ur," *Mesopotamian Civilizations*, Volume 1

All of these elephant-people also seem reminiscent of the small white elephant from Buddhist beliefs, that artificially impregnated Siddhartha's mother, and then ten months later preformed the cesarean section to bring Siddhartha into the world. Of course, no one, other than some Buddhists believe the Buddha was delivered by a small white elephant surgeon what came down from the sky, but, the point is that the belief in a small elephant-man persisted to at least the time of Siddhartha, circa 600 BC, and to our modern age, if one counts Ganesha, and it would be hard not to. Nevertheless, the Oxford Palette clearly depicts an upright-walking and clothed elephant-man circa 5500 BC ULT, so this icon has been around for a long time, and across a large area.

The Bull-Man

The various archaic belief systems across the region also all shared the icon of the bull-man. This bull-man is found on seals from both the Indus Valley and Sumer and was identically depicted. This Bull-man is identified as Enkidu in Sumerian stories, which would date his life, if he lived, to circa 7600 BC ULT in the Sumerian King List.

Above are two seals depicting the Bull-man fighting with animals. The left image is from the Indus Valley, and the right is a depiction of Enkidu from the Akkadian Empire, circa 3885 to 3700 BC ULT.

This bull-man also shows up in several other cultures, most notably the Greek Minotaur story, which is itself set in the ancient Minoan Civilization. The Egyptians had several bovine deities, including including the Apis Bulls themselves, who were venerated much as cattle continue to be venerated in India today. The most prominent Egyptian Bull-man god of the Old Kingdom was Amen, also transliterated as Amon or Amun, the creator god who breathed life into the world, a story that was later incorporated into Jewish Torah, and continued to be believed by many Christians to this day. Ironically while both Jews and Christians have forgotten who the god was that breathed life into the world, they continue to say his name at the end of prayers and claim it means something different, and in completely unrelated to the original god from the story.

In the Middle East, and well as other regions of the world, the horned-god became synonymous with evil. This transition seems to have happened over a long period of time, with some horned-beings already seen as evil in the epics of India, and Bacchus, the last horned-gods in the Greco-Roman Civilization being officially restricted in 186 BC, and later banned with the rest of the old gods when Christianity became the state religion in the 4th century AD. In the Sanskrit epics, these horned beings were called rakshasas, and like the nagas, were depicted as living in generally human-like societies. One simple explanation for these 'peoples' were different and conflicting religions, one which venerated the bull, and another with venerated the snake, both of which were viewed as alien by the original authors of the epics. Whatever they were, like the nagas, some individuals fought on the side of the heroes, and others fought on the side of the enemies. In the *Ramayana*, the rakshasas served as an army for Ravana, while in the later *Mahabharta* individuals fought on both sides, and the most powerful warrior on the side of

Arjuna and Krishna was a rakshasa called Gha-totkacha.

Unlike the nagas, the rakshasas were depicted as having many magical powers, although descriptions vary by the epic. Generally, rakshasas were illusionists, who could make themselves appear as giants, or look like humans. While this may be a later addition to the epics in the Classical era, it probably isn't as the ancient Sumerian *Epic of Gilgamesh* ascribes similar shape-changing abilities to Ninsun, the mother of King Gilgamesh. Ninsun, originally named Gula, was another cow-goddess, who also had the ability to appear in human form. While this may be a later mythical aspect added to the Gilgamesh story, it dates back to the Akkadian era in Mesopotamian history, circa 3885 to 3700 BC ULT, which would place it in the Harappan 3C Phase, at the same point in time as the seals that depict the Bull-man, which have been found in both the ruins of the Indus Valley Civilization and the Akkadian Empire.

Conclusion

All evidence for the existence of the Indo-European cultures is linguistic, religious, genetic, or related to horses. There is no clear evidence of an Indo-European type of pottery, form of writing, or architectural style. The ancient Greeks believed they were related to ancient Persians and Indo-Aryans based on various linguistic and cultural similarities. This idea resurfaced in the European colonial era when Europeans discovered the similarities between Sanskrit, Avestan, and modern South Asian and European languages. This was followed by the discovery that many of the pre-Christian deities of Europe appear to be variants of Vedic gods.

Several similar animal-human gods have been documented across Egypt, Southern Asia, Eastern Asia, and the Mesoamerica, however, they are generally not considered proof of ancient contact as animals are everywhere. Naturally, this does not explain the animal-gods that exist outside the region the animals are indigenous to. While the collection of similar animalistic iconography across the ancient world may not be evidence of widespread civilization of missionary work in ancient times, it is part of the larger map of human pre-history, which includes linguistics, genetics, and written records.

The traditional timelines developed by Indologists in the 1920s and 1930s have already been generally abandoned by modern Indologists, at least as far as the civilization being founded around 3300 BC, when James Henry Breasted claimed Egypt was founded. Ruins dating back to over 8000 BC are now accepted within Indology, much like in Assyriology, where some ancient Sumerian cities are believed date back to that time. However, unlike the Assyriologist, the Indologists are willing to accept that the early sites like Mehgarh and Bhirrana are related to the Indus Valley Civilization. Assyriologist still clings to Conventional Mesopotamian Timeline, meaning the Sumerians cities were built by someone else, who then lived in them, and developed the Sumerian pictographic script, before suddenly disappearing and being instantaneously replaced with an identical 'Sumerian' people circa 3100 BC, which is coincidentally when Egyptologists claim the Egyptian civilization spontaneously appeared along the Nile.

Fortunately, the Nazis lost World War II, and therefore there is no academic discipline of Aryanology with its timeline built around political ideology. The various disciplines that have been intersecting in the field of Indo-European origins since World War II have primarily been focused on the underlying study of linguistics, comparative-mythology, palegenetics, archaeology in Central Asia and the Eurasian Steppes. As these fields of study are largely independent of the ancient civilizations of Egypt and Mesopotamia, they are generally not subject to the conventional timelines developed in the early 1900s, which are themselves based on the biblical timeline and not the records of the ancient Egyptians or Mesopotamians. This freedom from these restrictions has allowed some very diverse theories to have been proposed for almost every aspect of Indo-European origins.

Unfortunately, the conventional timelines restrict the study of Indo-European origins and migrations in a few key ways:

1) The sudden appearance of the Indo-Aryan Mitanni in the Middle East, circa 1500 BC CMT, would force the Indo-Aryans have been existing at that time, and speaking a Rigvedic or Mantra Language dialect. Linguistically, this should not have existed so recently, but several thousand years earlier. In the Universal Long Timeline, there is no conflict as the Mitanni Empire came into existence circa 2967 BC, at the time linguists believe Rigvedic should have been giving way to Mantra Language, as the early Indo-Aryans spread out from their homeland using the horses and wagons they'd invented in Eurasian Steppes. This technology did not arrive in Mesopotamia in 1500s, but were already in use by 2600 BC, according to the Standard of Ur. Nevertheless, the Mesopotamians adopted Rigvedic and Mantra Language terminology for horses, harnesses, chariots, axles, and a number of related terms. How did they do this in the conventional timelines without time-travel? In the conventional timelines, they adopted terms from a language that would not exist for almost a thousand years!

2) The Hyksos invasion of Egypt is another problem for the conventional timeline of Indo-Aryan studies. According to Egyptologists, the Hyksos were a Semitic people with a Hurrian nobility, which invaded Egypt from Syria around 1674 BC CET, while Assyriologists have no records of the Hyksos anywhere in the Middle East. Some of these Hyksos had Indo-Aryan names, and they introduced Indo-

Aryan terminology to Egypt for horses and chariots, a over 800 years after the Sumerians had horses and chariots, but almost 200 years before the same terminology was adopted by the Babylonians or Assyrians, which in theory, the Hyksos should have encountered as they passed through the Middle East. The existence of a Semitic population, with a Hurrian nobility, using Indo-Aryan terminology, cannot be accounted for in the Middle East, or anywhere, circa 1674 BC, however, still requires the Rigvedic or Mantra Language Indo-Aryans to have existed around that time, for the Hyksos to be using their terminology. Again, this is a problem for linguists as those dialects, and event the Samhita Prose dialect that followed should all have been obsolete by that point.

3) The Conventional Mesopotamian Timeline also defines the Conventional Harappan Timeline through several Harappan artifacts that have been found in Kish, Nippur, and Susa. These artifacts correspond to the Harappan 1, Harappan 3B, and Harappan 3C phases, which spans the majority of Harappan history. As these artifacts are dated to Mesopotamian dynasties between 2900 and 1788 BC, early Indologists used these dates to create the Conventional Harappan Timeline. This timeline simply does not fit the evidence found within India and Pakistan, and therefore the original CHT had the Mehrgarh Phases added to it, which extend the CHT back to 7000 BC. However, older ruins have been found in the region, which will force the CHT to be adjusted by back another 1000 to 2000 years. The CHT also conflicts with the established date of iron

smelting within India, which is now known to have begun by 2400 BC. No iron artifacts have been found within the ruins of the Indus Valley Civilization, yet, this civilization was neighboring an iron-smelting civilization of 1100 years? This is simply not possible. The Indus Valley Civilization must precede the iron-working civilizations of the Ganges and southern India, or they would have adopted the technology themselves. Forcing the Indus Valley Civilization to be as late as the CHT requires, means that the Indo-Aryans could not have arrived in India until around 1300 BC, and therefore the Sanskrit language must have gone through all the stages of development through Rigvedic, Mantra Language, Samhita Prose, Brahmana Prose, and Sutra Language, developing into Classical Sanskrit by 500 BC, meaning that an estimated 4000 thousands of years of linguistic development had to have taken place in only 800 years.

These various inconsistencies do not occur in the Universal Long Timeline, where the Sanskrit dialects had thousands of years to develop as the Indo-Aryans migrated from Ukraine, east into the Steppes of Russia and Kazakhstan, and south to the Oxus Civilization, before migrating south into Pakistan and India. The Indo-Aryans then spread out from the steppes around 3000 BC, occupying Babylonia circa 3013 BC, establishing the Mitanni Empire circa 2967 BC, whose descendants the Hyksos then invaded Egypt in 2533 BC, introducing the horse, and chariot technology, shortly after they were first documented in Babylonia circa 2600 BC.

The Indus Valley Civilization is generally regarded as having been a Dravidian-speaking civilization, and the genetic evidence of widespread but low percentages of M-DNA common to the Dravidian people, across South Asia, as well Iran, Arabia, and the Mediterranean Sea. If only the CHT is considered, the existence of the M-DNA implies that the Dravidian population spread widely through the region several thousand years before the Indus Valley Civilization was founded, however, in the ULT this genetic material spread through the cultures of Mesopotamia, Egypt, and the Mediterranean during the height of the Indus Valley Civilization, before the subsequent arrival of the Indo-European M-DNA from the north.

While Indologists generally want to abandon the conventional timelines and will have to in the next decade, as far too many Harappan-like ancient ruins have been found in India, Pakistan, and off the coast, that clearly date to several thousand years before the CHT. Additionally, the discovery of massive and widespread iron smelting in India proves the Indus Valley Civilization could not have existed as late as the CHT requires. Unfortunately, developing a separate timeline for the Indus Valley Civilization would imply that the conventional timelines of Mesopotamia and Egypt are wrong, and so Indologists are delaying the inevitable.

Also Available

Broken Timelines – Book 1: Egypt

Broken Timelines – Book 2: Mesopotamia

Broken Timelines – Book 3: The Indo-Europeans and the Harappans